VOCABULARY

Meaning and Message

Number 1

Stella Sands

Fearon/Janus
Belmont, California

Simon & Schuster Supplementary Education Group

CONTENTS

Copyright © 1992 by Fearon/Janus, a division of Simon & Schuster Supplementary Education Group, 500 Harbor Boulevard, Belmont, California 94002. All rights reserved. Permission is hereby granted to reproduce materials in this book for noncommercial classroom use.

ISBN 0–8224–9476–0

Printed in the United States of America.

BA

10 9 8 7 6

Cover Illustrator: Hank Osuna
Cover Designer: Dianne Platner
Illustrators: James Balkovek, Rick Hackney, James McConnell,
Margaret Sanfilippo, Frances Thompson

Reading on Your Own

Name _____ Date _____

As you read this story, think about the meaning of each highlighted word.

Your Five Senses

What memory stands out most in your mind? Is it of seeing a friend for the first time in years and hearing his or her voice? Maybe it's the smell of hot apple pie or the **taste** of homemade bread at your grandmother's house. Perhaps it's the touch of a baby's **hand** on your cheek.

Whatever your strongest memory, you have it because of one of your five **senses.** These senses are sight, taste, smell, hearing, and touch.

Which of your senses do you think you could not live without?

Some people think that sight is their most **important** sense. Without **eyes** to see, they wouldn't be able to watch their children playing. They couldn't view a soccer game. They wouldn't see the colors of fall leaves. They could never look closely at a butterfly's wings.

Others think that hearing is the one sense they couldn't do without. Without **ears** to hear, they wouldn't know the **sounds** of their loved ones' voices. They couldn't listen to their favorite music. They wouldn't be able to enjoy the morning songs of birds.

The sense of smell is important to many people. They want to be able to **breathe** in the aroma of flowers. They want to smell barbecued chicken and corn bread.

To others, the sense of taste matters most. These people want their **tongues** to taste spicy sauces and sour pickles. They want to enjoy sweet ice cream, tart apples, and salty pretzels.

The sense of touch is crucial to many people. If their **skin** couldn't feel, they wouldn't sense the warmth of sunlight or the chill of a cool breeze.

Our senses give us information about the world we live in. And they help us build a world of memories.

Tell about a strong memory you have. Include details about one or more of your five senses.

_____

_____

_____

Vocabulary: Meaning and Message © Fearon/Janus Publishers

Lesson 1, Exercise 2
Using Context

Name _____ Date _____

Imagine reading a letter from your friend Sally. She writes, "I found a picture of us together when we were five years old. We don't look great, but I couldn't *discard* the picture. I'll send it to you for your birthday."

Suppose you don't know the meaning of the word *discard*. You could stop reading and look it up in a dictionary. Or you could try to figure out the word's meaning from how it is being used. The other words and sentences can give you clues. These surrounding words and sentences are called the *context*. By looking for context clues, you can often figure out a word's meaning.

In the above example, you might have guessed that *discard* means "to throw away."

Use the words in the box to complete the sentences below. Write the letter for that word on the line.

a. taste	c. hands	e. senses	g. important	i. eyes
b. ears	d. sound	f. breathe	h. tongues	j. skin

1. Barbara wanted to wear jewelry, so she had her _____ pierced.

2. Try this hot chili if you like the _____ of spicy food.

3. In many cities, the air we _____ may be harmful to our health.

4. Many animals can reach far out of their mouths with their _____ .

5. You find out about the world through your five _____ .

6. Locked boxes are good places to keep _____ papers.

7. When I stay in the sun too long, my _____ burns.

8. Croaking frogs make a noisy _____ .

9. Many owls have very large _____ .

10. Most married people wear their wedding rings on their left _____ .

Vocabulary Development: Idioms

Name _____ Date _____

Idioms are groups of words that don't mean exactly what they say. For example, if someone says she is "all ears," that doesn't mean she is made only of ears. It means she is listening carefully.

There are many idioms in the English language. By knowing their meanings, you'll be able to understand and speak with a wide range of people. So *put your nose to the grindstone* and learn some idioms. It will keep you from *putting your foot in your mouth*.

Here are ten idioms. Each one is followed by its meaning and a sentence. On the line, use the idiom in a sentence of your own.

1. **by the skin of one's teeth**—just barely

   John passed the test by the skin of his teeth.

   _____

   _____

2. **to keep an eye on**—to watch carefully

   If you're a babysitter, you must keep an eye on the children.

   _____

   _____

3. **to see eye to eye**—to agree completely

   Patricia and Tom don't see eye to eye on the best way to get the work done.

   _____

   _____

4. **to catch one's eye**—to get someone to pay attention

   I tried to catch Joey's eye as he walked into class.

   _____

   _____

Vocabulary: Meaning and Message © Fearon/Janus Publishers

Vocabulary Development: Idioms

Name _____ Date _____

5. **to hand down**—to give something, to pass on, especially from older people to younger people

   That watch was handed down to me by my grandfather.

   _____

   _____

6. **on hand**—ready for use

   After the race, there was water on hand for the runners.

   _____

   _____

7. **hands down**—easily

   We won the game hands down.

   _____

   _____

8. **to play by ear**—to play music without having to read the notes

   Yolanda played many well-known songs on the piano by ear.

   _____

   _____

9. **be all ears**—listen carefully

   When the test results were announced, Hank was all ears.

   _____

   _____

10. **lend an ear**—pay attention

    The teacher said to the class, "Lend an ear and you'll learn about Paul Revere's ride."

    _____

    _____

Puzzle

Name _____ Date _____

The letters of each word below are not in their correct order. Rearrange the letters to form the words in the box. Then use each word in a sentence of your own.

breathe	ears	eyes	hand	important
senses	skin	sounds	taste	tongue

1. a h d n _____ _____

   _____

2. r s a e _____ _____

   _____

3. y e e s _____ _____

   _____

4. n i k s _____ _____

   _____

5. s t a e t _____ _____

   _____

6. e g u o n t _____ _____

   _____

7. n d u o s s _____ _____

   _____

8. s n s e e s _____ _____

   _____

9. e b r t h a e _____ _____

   _____

10. r t a p o n t i m _____ _____

   _____

Vocabulary: Meaning and Message © Fearon/Janus Publishers

Lesson 1, Exercise 5
Dictionary Skills: Alphabetizing

Name _____ Date _____

Dictionaries are very useful books. They tell you the meanings of words. They also show you how to say and spell words. The exercises below will help you learn how to use a dictionary.

The words in a dictionary are arranged in alphabetical order. This means that they appear in the same order as the letters of the alphabet. Words beginning with the letter *a* come before words beginning with the letter *b*. Words beginning with the letter *c* come before words beginning with the letter *d*, and so on. Words beginning with *a*, *b*, and *c* are found at the beginning of the dictionary. Words beginning with *x*, *y*, and *z* are found at the end. Knowing how the words are arranged makes it easy to look them up.

A. Read each group of words below. Then arrange the words in alphabetical order. To do this, write a number beside each word. The first one has been done for you as an example.

1. hand __2__	2. senses _____	3. sound _____
eye __1__	breathe _____	taste _____
skin __3__	tongue _____	ears _____

Of course, many words begin with the same first letter. How do you know which words come first in the dictionary? It depends on the words' second letters. For example, *smell* and *see* both begin with *s*. But, the second letter in *see* is *e*. And *e* comes before *m*, the second letter in *smell*. So the word *see* comes before the word *smell*.

B. Number these words in alphabetical order.

1. eyes _____	2. taste _____	3. skin _____
ears _____	tongue _____	senses _____
every _____	they _____	sound _____

Vocabulary: Meaning and Message © Fearon/Janus Publishers

Writing on Your Own

Name _____ Date _____

A. **Which sense do you think is most important: sight, taste, smell, hearing, or touch? Write the senses below in their order of importance to you. The sense you write next to the number 1 should be the sense you think is most important. The sense you write next to the number 5 should be the sense you think is least important.**

1. _____

2. _____

3. _____

4. _____

5. _____

B. **Explain why you chose the sense you did as the most important.**

_____

_____

_____

_____

_____

Vocabulary: Meaning and Message © Fearon/Janus Publishers

Lesson 1, Exercise 7
Test

Name _____ Date _____

Choose the best word to complete each sentence. Write the letter on the line.

1. I keep my passport in a safe place. It is one of the most _____ items I own.

   A. friendly   B. beautiful   C. important   D. extra

2. After being in the city, it felt wonderful to _____ the fresh country air.

   A. explain   B. compare   C. fasten   D. breathe

3. Most people wear rings on the fingers of their _____. But some people wear rings in their noses.

   A. faces   B. hands   C. legs   D. doors

4. While flying through the sky, a hawk can see things on the ground with its sharp _____ .

   A. ears   B. eyes   C. hands   D. tongue

5. The ocean waves made a loud _____ when striking the shore.

   A. sound   B. figure   C. heard   D. flight

6. To some people, lima beans don't _____ very good.

   A. steer   B. touch   C. stare   D. taste

7. Very loud sounds can hurt your _____ .

   A. eyes   B. ears   C. senses   D. hands

8. Ian thinks sight is the one _____ he couldn't live without.

   A. sense   B. time   C. state   D. important

9. To catch insects, frogs stick out their _____ .

   A. hands   B. ears   C. senses   D. tongues

10. As people age, their _____ begins to wrinkle.

   A. shoulder   B. step   C. skin   D. chin

Reading on Your Own

Name _____ Date _____

As you read this story, think about the meaning of each highlighted word.

Have a Great Trip!

Imagine you have just won a contest. Your prize is a trip to anywhere in the world. Where will you go? What form of **transportation** will you use to get there?

China is an interesting place to visit. You could fly there in an **airplane.** The ride through the skies takes a long time from the United States. From New York, for example, it takes about 24 hours! In China, you could walk along the Great Wall. It was built over 2,000 years ago. The wall is high and very long. It was built to keep China safe from its enemies to the north.

You might want to visit to Egypt. There you could take a bus to see the pyramids. Pyramids are very large buildings in which kings and queens were buried.

You could also visit Europe. Once you got there, you could **travel** by train to many different countries. You could see the Eiffel Tower in Paris, France, or the Leaning Tower of Pisa in Italy. You could go to Spain and see a bullfight.

If you want to stay in the United States, you might like to visit the Empire State Building or the World Trade Center in New York City. You can get to them by taking a **subway** train. Subways run along tracks underground. They hold many people in separate cars. Street **traffic** doesn't slow down the subways. If you don't like traveling under the ground, you could ride a **bicycle.** A bicycle doesn't need gas or an engine. It needs only leg power. It can go places that larger **vehicles** can't. But if you wish, you could pay a **taxi** driver to take you where you want to go.

You might decide to travel to San Francisco, California. Going up that city's many hills on a bicycle would be hard work. It would be less tiring to ride a **motorcycle.** Like a bicycle, a motorcycle has two wheels. But it also has an engine, which makes getting up hills a lot easier. In San Francisco you could also take a **ferry** to the island of Alcatraz. Alcatraz is the site of a famous prison that is now closed.

What form of transportation do you think you'd like most? Why?

_____

_____

_____

Vocabulary: Meaning and Message © Fearon/Janus Publishers

Lesson 2, Exercise 2
Using Context

Name _____ Date _____

Use the words in the box to complete the sentences below.

motorcycle	ferry	airplane	traveled	subway
bicycles	taxi	vehicles	traffic	transportation

My friend Fran visited me and my parents last summer. Fran had never been to Boston before. She flew here from Chicago. The _____ arrived on time.

On our first day together, Fran and I packed a picnic lunch. We put it in our backpacks. Then we got on two _____ and pedaled through the city. Going up Beacon Hill was hard, but we did it.

On another day, we took a bus trip along with 20 other people to two nearby towns. Because there wasn't much _____ on the streets, we got to them pretty quickly. The bus driver showed us the towns of Lexington and Concord. The first battle of the Revolutionary War was fought there in 1775. We also visited Salem. About 20 people were killed there in the 1600s because they were thought to be witches!

One sunny morning, Fran and I went to the island of Nantucket. The _____ ride over the water took about two hours. It was so much fun! We both decided that this was our favorite means of _____. On Nantucket, we swam and played volleyball. Then we took a nap on the beach. Our sleep was broken by two people riding a _____ on a nearby street. We would have missed the ferry if the loud engine hadn't awakened us. We called a _____ to take us to the boat. The ride cost us five dollars.

On Fran's last day here, we _____ downtown by bus to go shopping. There were so many _____ on the streets that we almost wished we'd stayed home. A faster way to get around Boston is to go underground in the _____.

Vocabulary: Meaning and Message © Fearon/Janus Publishers

Vocabulary Development: Plural Nouns

Name _____ Date _____

A **noun** is a word that names a person, place, or thing. Your own name is a noun. A noun is the name of anything you can touch. But when we say "thing," we are including ideas, feelings, qualities, and events. So nouns also name things you can't touch. The word *truth* is a noun.

A singular noun names one person, place, or thing. *Car* and *train* are singular nouns. So are *joke, fear, loyalty,* and *rally*.

A plural noun names more than one person, place, or thing. *Cars* and *trains* are plural nouns. So are *jokes, fears, loyalties,* and *rallies*.

It is easy to form plural nouns from singular nouns. In most cases, you make a singular noun plural simply by adding an *s* to it.

Singular nouns:	contest	place	hour	pyramid
Plural nouns:	contests	places	hours	pyramids

A. Write the plural forms of these singular nouns.

Singular nouns:	building	queen	train
Plural nouns:	_____	_____	_____

The plurals of some singular nouns are formed in a different way. It helps to know the rules for how to do this. Nouns that end in *y,* for instance, have their own rules. If you remember these rules, you'll know how to make them plural whenever you want to.

To form the plural of a singular noun that ends in a vowel and a *y,* do what you do with most nouns. Just add an *s.* (Remember that the vowels are *a, e, i, o,* and *u.*)

Singular nouns:	key	tray	joy	guy
Plural nouns:	keys	trays	joys	guys

Vocabulary: Meaning and Message © Fearon/Janus Publishers

Lesson 2, Exercise 3

Vocabulary Development: Plural Nouns

Name _____ Date _____

To form the plural of a singular noun that ends in a consonant and a *y*, change the *y* to *i* and add *es*. (The consonants are all the letters of the alphabet except *a, e, i, o,* and *u*.)

Singular nouns: sky penny rally party
Plural nouns: skies pennies rallies parties

B. The words in each list below form their plural in the same way. Follow the example and write the plural next to each word.

Singular	Plural
1. motorcycle	motorcycles (just add *s*)
2. airplane	_____
3. bicycle	_____
4. taxi	_____
5. vehicle	_____
6. sound	_____
7. sense	_____
8. way	ways (add *s*)
9. subway	_____
10. trolley	_____
11. play	_____
12. turkey	_____
13. monkey	_____
14. boy	_____
15. enemy	enemies (change *y* to *i* and add *es*)
16. fly	_____
17. ferry	_____
18. pony	_____
19. cherry	_____
20. duty	_____
21. blueberry	_____

Puzzle

Name _____   Date _____

Here are four road signs. Look at each sign and then read its meaning below.

A. Let the other car go.

B. Go slowly; be careful.

C. People may be crossing the street here.

D. Take a different route.

Choose the best sign to answer each of these questions. Write the letter of the sign on the line.

1. You are driving in your car and you see that the road ahead is closed. What sign tells you where to go? _____

2. Two cars are coming from different directions. If they keep going, they will meet at the same spot. Which sign tells you which car should go first? _____

3. The road ahead is bumpy and narrow. Which sign tells you to slow down? _____

4. Which sign tells you where it is safe to walk across the street? _____

Dictionary Skills: Alphabetizing

Name _____ Date _____

A. Put these words in alphabetical order. If you need help, look back at page 9. Write the words on the lines.

vehicle	bicycle	airplane	ferry
subway	taxi	motorcycle	traffic

1. _____   5. _____

2. _____   6. _____

3. _____   7. _____

4. _____   8. _____

If the first two letters of words are the same, the alphabetical order of the words depends on the third letters. For example, the words *car* and *cab* both begin with the letters *ca.* Look to the third letters of each word—*r* and *b*—to decide which word comes first. Since *b* comes before *r,* the word *cab* comes before *car.*

B. Put the words in each list below in alphabetical order. Write 1 next to the word that comes first. Write 2 next to the word that comes next, and so on.

1. airplane _____   4. ferry _____

   aid _____   fence _____

   aim _____   feather _____

                          fell _____

2. bicycle _____

   bite _____   5. motorcycle _____

   big _____   movie _____

                          more _____

3. traffic _____   most _____

   treat _____   money _____

   trick _____

   true _____

Writing on Your Own

Name _____ Date _____

A. Five vehicles are named below. In one or two sentences, tell why you think you would or would not like to use each one.

1. **airplane**

   _____

   _____

2. **ferry**

   _____

   _____

3. **taxi**

   _____

   _____

4. **subway**

   _____

   _____

5. **motorcycle**

   _____

   _____

B. Suppose you worked in a bicycle shop. What might you say to get someone to buy a bike?

   _____

   _____

   _____

   _____

   _____

Vocabulary: Meaning and Message © Fearon/Janus Publishers

Lesson 2, Exercise 7
Test

Name _____ Date _____

Choose the best word to complete each sentence.

1. We couldn't hear the street noises while riding underground in the _____.

   A. ferry   B. taxi   C. subway   D. motorcycle

2. One way to get to Staten Island is to take a _____ over the waters of New York Bay.

   A. subway   B. motorcycle   C. bicycle   D. ferry

3. Pete's legs hurt after he had ridden a _____ for five hours.

   A. taxi   B. ferry   C. bicycle   D. traffic

4. We were late getting here because of the _____ on the roads.

   A. bicycles   B. traffic   C. ferries   D. motorcycles

5. To get from California to New York takes about five hours by _____.

   A. airplane   B. ferry   C. motorcycle   D. traffic

6. Many people do not like the noise of _____.

   A. travel   B. bicycles   C. ferries   D. motorcycles

7. Riding in an airplane is my favorite form of _____.

   A. traffic   B. transportation   C. ferry   D. airplane

8. Roland had only $5.00 in his pocket. Luckily the _____ ride cost him only $3.50. That included the tip for the driver.

   A. airplane   B. motorcycle   C. taxi   D. travel

9. Traveling on steep mountain roads is difficult for some _____.

   A. vehicles   B. travel   C. airplanes   D. traffic

10. I would very much like to _____ to India some day.

   A. subway   B. traffic   C. transportation   D. travel

Vocabulary: Meaning and Message © Fearon/Janus Publishers

Reading on Your Own

Name _____ Date _____

As you read this story, think about the meaning of each highlighted word.

Lights Out!

In 1965, there was a blackout along most of the northeastern United States and in parts of Canada. It lasted from November 9th to 10th. All the lights went out. There was no **electricity.** All the electrically powered **appliances** stopped working.

Some people were stuck in **elevators** in tall buildings. They may have been on their way to a high floor. They may have been going down to a ground floor. When the blackout happened, all the elevators stopped. Some of the cars stopped between floors. The lights in them went out. People were stuck with other people in small dark spaces.

Some people were home at the time cooking dinner on electric **stoves.** They may have been frying vegetables on one burner and boiling water for spaghetti on another. In the **ovens,** they may have had cakes baking. All of a sudden, no heat came from the burners. The ovens stopped working.

In the **refrigerators,** they may have had milk and juice that they'd been planning to drink with dinner. When the power went out, the motors in the refrigerators stopped. If the electricity didn't come back on soon, everything would spoil.

Toasters stopped warming bread. Clothes **washers** and **dryers** stopped cleaning clothes. **Dishwashers** no longer cleaned and washed the dishes.

The blackout lasted only two days. Those who are old enough to remember it have strong memories of that time. It wasn't easy to do many of the things people normally do almost without thinking of them. But the blackout did point out how much everyone depended on electricity.

Imagine that there has just been a blackout. Which electrical device do you think you are going to miss most? Tell why.

_____

_____

_____

Vocabulary: Meaning and Message © Fearon/Janus Publishers

Lesson 3, Exercise 2
Using Context

Name _____ Date _____

Choose a word from the box to replace the highlighted words in each sentence. Write the letter for that word on the line.

a. toaster	c. refrigerator	e. dishwasher	g. oven	i. washer
b. stove	d. electricity	f. appliances	h. dryer	j. elevator

1. At breakfast, Jed ate a muffin he had heated in the **small device for warming bread.** _____

2. After riding our bikes in the rain, we put our clothes into the **machine that takes the wetness out of clothes.** _____

3. When the electricity went off, none of the **machines or small devices that do a particular job** worked. _____

4. We rode to the 30th floor in the **small room that takes people from one level to another in buildings.** _____

5. After dinner, we put the dishes into the **machine that gets dishes, pots and pans, and silverware clean.** We didn't have to wash them by hand. _____

6. I put the cheese into the **large box with an electrical cooling system** so that it wouldn't spoil. _____

7. The pie has been baking in the **enclosed part of our stove** for over an hour. _____

8. The onions are frying on the **large piece of equipment that has burners on it, as well as an enclosed cooking area.** _____

9. My hair dryer is powered by **a form of energy that can run motors.** _____

10. After playing on the muddy field, we put our clothes into the **machine that gets clothes clean.** _____

Vocabulary Development: Multiple Meanings

Name _____ Date _____

Billy was reading a newspaper story. It reported that people were expected to *jam* the beaches that weekend. Billy thought that somehow people were going to spread *jam* all over the beaches.

Have you ever been in a situation like Billy's? Sometimes the words you're reading seem to make no sense at all. Could it be that the author is using a word with more than one meaning?

The word *jam,* for example, has several meanings:

first meaning:	to completely fill or block
second meaning:	to wedge
third meaning:	to squeeze into a tight space to prevent movement
fourth meaning:	a sweet food made by boiling fruit and sugar until it becomes thick

Many words do have more than one meaning. Sometimes you have to figure out which one a writer is using. To do that, look at the other words and the sentences around the word for clues. If Billy doesn't read anything about food, he knows the newspaper story probably isn't about the jam people eat.

Vocabulary Development: Multiple Meanings

Name _____ Date _____

A. Each highlighted word has more than one meaning. On the line, write the meaning used in the sentence. If you need help, use a dictionary.

1. My **toast** with butter and strawberry jam was delicious.

   _____

2. The wedding guests offered a **toast** to the bride and groom.

   _____

3. Many people wash their clothes by **hand**.

   _____

4. The **hands** of the clock are both on 12.

   _____

5. At the end of the show, the actors were given a big **hand**.

   _____

B. The words below have more than one meaning. Read the meanings and then use each word in a sentence of your own.

1. **mount:** first meaning: to climb; to go up

   _____

   second meaning: a horse or other animal used for riding

   _____

2. **chest:** first meaning: the front, upper part of the body

   _____

   second meaning: a large, solid box often with a lid and lock used for holding things

   _____

3. **fly:** first meaning: an insect with wings

   _____

   second meaning: to travel by airplane

   _____

Puzzle

Name _____   Date _____

**Use the clues to to help you complete the crossword puzzle.
The answers can be found in the box.**

electricity	oven	refrigerator	toaster	elevator
appliance	stove	dishwasher	dryer	washer

Across
4. a small room that carries people and things from one floor to another in a building
5. a large metal object used for cooking food
6. a large box with an electric cooling system; used to store food
8. a small machine that browns bread
9. a machine that cleans pots, pans, and dishes

Down
1. the enclosed part of a stove
2. a machine that takes the wetness out of clothing
3. a machine that gets clothes clean
4. a form of energy that runs televisions, radios, and other items
7. a device that does a specific job

Vocabulary: Meaning and Message © Fearon/Janus Publishers

Dictionary Skills: Alphabetizing

Name _____ Date _____

Many words begin with the same three first letters. For example, *heater, hear,* and *heavy* all begin with *hea.* How do you know which of these words comes first in a dictionary? Look at the fourth letter of each word: *t, r,* and *v.* Which letter comes first in alphabetical order?

The answer is *r.* Therefore, the word *hear* comes first. The next word would be *heater,* because the *t* in *heater* comes before the *v* in *heavy.* The last word is *heavy,* because *v* comes after both *r* and *t.*

Put the words in each list in alphabetical order. Write 1 next to the word that comes first. Write 2 next to the word that comes second, and so on.

1. refrigerator _____
   refugee _____
   reform _____

2. stove _____
   story _____
   stone _____

3. washer _____
   wasp _____
   waste _____

4. hanker _____
   hang _____
   hand _____

5. skip _____
   skin _____
   skit _____

6. disobey _____
   dishwasher _____
   distant _____

7. elegant _____
   elevator _____
   electricity _____
   elephant _____

8. south _____
   soup _____
   souvenir _____
   sour _____
   sound _____

9. travel _____
   traffic _____
   transportation _____
   trade _____
   train _____

10. subway _____
    subject _____
    subscribe _____
    subtract _____
    submarine _____

Vocabulary: Meaning and Message © Fearon/Janus Publishers

Writing on Your Own

Name _____ Date _____

Think of all the electrical devices you use every day. Which of them are most important to you? Tell why.

_____

_____

_____

_____

_____

_____

There are many new electrical products in the stores today. There are computers, video games, VCRs, answering machines, and many, many more. If you were going to buy one of them, which would it be? Why?

_____

_____

_____

_____

_____

Vocabulary: Meaning and Message © Fearon/Janus Publishers

Lesson 3, Exercise 7
Test

Name _____ Date _____

Choose the best word to complete each sentence.

1. The Sears Tower in Chicago, Illinois, is 110 stories high. You might not go to your office there if the _____ weren't working.

   A. appliances   B. elevators   C. dishwasher   D. stairs

2. I was warming some leftover pizza in the _____.

   A. refrigerator   B. washer   C. blackout   D. oven

3. We were heating milk for hot chocolate on top of the _____.

   A. appliances   B. dishwasher   C. toaster   D. stove

4. The fruit was cold because it had been in the _____.

   A. stove   B. appliance   C. refrigerator   D. elevator

5. All the traffic lights, as well as the streetlights, are powered by _____.

   A. dishwasher   B. senses   C. electricity   D. sounds

6. My bread burned because the _____ switch had broken.

   A. dryer   B. appliance   C. refrigerator   D. toaster

7. Joe put his dirty clothes into the _____.

   A. stove   B. elevator   C. refrigerator   D. washer

8. Put those dirty pots and pans into the _____.

   A. dryer   B. dishwasher   C. oven   D. elevator

9. Many people think that a blender is a useful kitchen _____.

   A. appliance   B. washer   C. food item   D. taste

10. I put the clean wet sheets into the _____.

    A. washer   B. dishwasher   C. appliance   D. dryer

Reading on Your Own

Name _____ Date _____

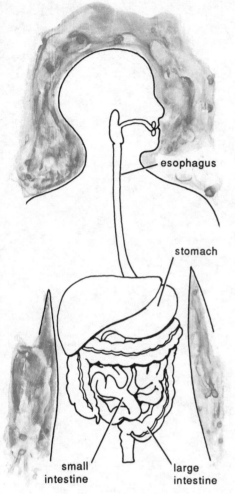

esophagus

stomach

small
intestine

large
intestine

**As you read this story, think about the meaning of each
highlighted word.**

Food for Thought

Imagine you are about to take the first bite of a turkey dinner.
You cut a piece of meat, put it on your fork, and raise the fork to
your **mouth**. But instead of simply enjoying the taste of the food,
you begin to wonder. "Where is the food going? How does it get
there? What happens along the way?"

After your front **teeth** bite into and cut the food, your back teeth
chew it. The food then mixes with the clear liquid called **saliva.**
Saliva makes your food soft and soggy. During this time, taste buds
on your tongue send messages to your brain. They tell you if you
are eating something salty, sour, sweet, or bitter.

Now you swallow. The food is forced by **muscles** down a long
tube known as the **esophagus.** The esophagus brings food to the
stomach. The stomach is an **organ** on the left side of the body.
Organs, such as the stomach, liver, heart, and eyes, perform specific
jobs for the body.

Food stays in your stomach three to six hours. During that time, it
mixes with **digestive** juices. These juices help break down the food.
They turn it into a thick souplike mass.

The soupy mixture passes into the small **intestine.** There it is
completely broken down into materials your body can use. These
then pass into your bloodstream.

In this way, your whole **body** is fed, and you are able to live and
grow. In adults, the small intestine is about 22 feet long. Food that
cannot be digested goes to the large intestine. The large intestine is
wider than the small intestine. But it is only about five feet long.
There, waste matter is stored after the water is taken out of it. Later
these wastes are passed out of the body.

Food takes from 10 to 20 hours to complete its journey through
your body. That seems like a very long time compared to the time it
takes to eat a meal.

**What happens to food right after you put it into your mouth?
Explain the first part of the food's journey, until the time you
swallow it.**

_____

_____

_____

Vocabulary: Meaning and Message © Fearon/Janus Publishers

Using Context

Name _____ Date _____

Use the words in the box to complete the sentences below.

body	intestines	muscles	saliva	teeth
stomach	digestive	esophagus	mouth	organs

1. Most adults chew their food with 32 _____.

2. Weight lifters often have huge arm _____.

3. The tongue and teeth are inside the _____.

4. The eyes, liver, and heart are three important
   _____ in the body.

5. The belly, or _____, is located between the
   esophagus and the small intestine.

6. In order for food to pass from your throat to your stomach, it
   must go down your _____.

7. Your mouth is wet because of the _____ there.

8. Bones, organs, muscles, joints, blood, and water are all inside
   your _____.

9. The breaking down of food so that it can be used by your body
   is called the _____ process.

10. Adults have about 27 feet of _____.

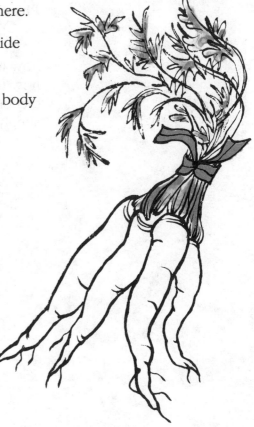

Vocabulary Development: Plural Nouns

Name _____ Date _____

On page 14, you learned about singular and plural nouns. As you remember, a singular noun names one person, place, or thing. A plural noun names more than one person, place, or thing. *Stomach* and *intestine* are singular nouns. *Stomachs* and *intestines* are plural nouns.

Many plurals are formed by adding *s* to the singular form of the noun. But some plural nouns are formed differently. In Lesson 1, you learned how to form the plurals of words ending in *y*. You saw that the plural of *subway* is *subways* and that the plural of *ferry* is *ferries*.

There are some nouns that change their "inside spelling" to form their plurals. For example, the plural of *mouse* is *mice*. The plural of *woman* is *women*. Here are a few more nouns that form their plurals in this way:

Singular nouns: man   foot   goose   die   tooth
Plural nouns: men   feet   geese   dice   teeth

Some nouns are spelled the same in both their singular and plural forms. Here are some examples:

Singular nouns: fish   deer   sheep   series
Plural nouns: fish   deer   sheep   series

It's a good idea to memorize such words. That way you'll know how to use them whenever you want to. But if you're ever not sure how to spell a plural, just look up the singular form of the word in a dictionary. If the plural form is not listed, that means it is formed simply by adding *s*.

Vocabulary: Meaning and Message © Fearon/Janus Publishers

Vocabulary Development: Plural Nouns

Name _____ Date _____

A. The words in the list below form their plurals in the same way. Follow the example and write the plural next to each singular word.

Singular	Plural
1. meal	meals (just add *s*)
2. mouth	_____
3. intestine	_____
4. muscle	_____
5. country	countries (change *y* to *i* and add *es*)
6. body	_____
7. treaty	_____
8. baby	_____

B. In each of these sentences, one noun is spelled incorrectly. Underline that noun in each sentence. Then rewrite the sentence with the noun spelled correctly.

1. The dentist took out two of my tooths.

   _____

2. All these young womans are in high school.

   _____

3. Cats are known to chase mouses.

   _____

4. We could hear the gooses honking overhead.

   _____

5. This game is played with two sets of dies.

   _____

6. Each men must speak for himself.

   _____

Puzzle

Name _____ Date _____

The words in the box can be found in the puzzle below. They may be written from right to left, left to right, top to bottom, or bottom to top. Find and circle each one. You may want to check off each word in the box after you have circled it. One word has been circled and checked as an example.

body	digestive	esophagus	✔ teeth	mouth	
muscles	saliva	intestine	stomach	organ	

```
b o c r e s o p h a g u s e l i
r b y d o t r h h (t e e t h) j n
a c d n x o g a m o o a o o z t
v l o h j m a g l r r g m p n e
i r b t u h n u t g a r a c t s
l p z u b i p s l m p a c u s t
a q p o s g b t f d m o h t h i
s i r m u s c l e s c o t a l n
a s a l p z d i g e s t i v e e
```

SNACK BAR

Vocabulary: Meaning and Message © Fearon/Janus Publishers

Dictionary Skills: Guide Words

Name _____ Date _____

In most dictionaries, guide words appear in **boldface** type at the top of each page. The guide words are there to help you to find the words you are looking up. The guide word on the top left side of the page is the first word defined on that page. The guide word on the top right side is the last word defined on that page. If the word you are looking for comes between the guide words alphabetically, it will be on that page.

For instance, *stomach* would be on a page that has the guide words **stitch** and **stone** at the top of it.

Stomach comes after the word *stitch*, because the *o* in *stomach* comes after the *i* in *stitch*. *Stomach* comes before the word *stone*, because the *m* in *stomach* comes before the *n* in *stone*.

Look up each of these words in a dictionary. Then write the guide words that appear at the top of that dictionary page.

Guide Words

1. intestine   _____   _____

2. mouth   _____   _____

3. tooth   _____   _____

4. esophagus   _____   _____

5. digestive   _____   _____

6. stomach   _____   _____

7. body   _____   _____

8. muscle   _____   _____

9. saliva   _____   _____

10. organ   _____   _____

11. liquid   _____   _____

12. message   _____   _____

Writing on Your Own

Name _____ Date _____

A. **Using your own words, finish the explanation you began on page 28. Tell what happens to food after you swallow it. Use these words when explaining the digestive process.**

intestine   stomach   body   esophagus   muscle

_____

_____

_____

_____

_____

_____

_____

_____

_____

_____

_____

_____

B. **What question or questions might you ask a doctor about digestion?**

_____

_____

_____

_____

_____

_____

Vocabulary: Meaning and Message © Fearon/Janus Publishers

Lesson 4, Exercise 7
Test

Name _____ Date _____

Choose the best word to complete each sentence.

1. When raising weights, weight lifters use arm, leg, and back _____.

   A. weights   B. intestines   C. muscles   D. organs

2. Food gets to your stomach by going down your _____.

   A. digestive   B. esophagus   C. body   D. organ

3. The process of breaking down food so that it can be used by the body is called the _____ process.

   A. muscle   B. esophagus   C. intestine   D. digestive

4. The liquid in your mouth that helps make your food easier to swallow is _____.

   A. digestive   B. organ   C. saliva   D. esophagus

5. Most chewing is done with the back _____.

   A. muscles   B. organs   C. intestines   D. teeth

6. After food leaves the esophagus, it travels to the _____.

   A. muscles   B. stomach   C. body   D. organ

7. Food that passes through the walls of the small _____ is changed into materials the body can use.

   A. stomach   B. intestine   C. organs   D. esophagus

8. For humans 98.6° F is the normal _____ temperature.

   A. muscle   B. body   C. digestive   D. teeth

9. The dentist said, "Open your _____ wide."

   A. mouth   B. organ   C. esophagus   D. intestine

10. The ear is the _____ for hearing.

    A. muscle   B. organ   C. body   D. intestine

Vocabulary: Meaning and Message © Fearon/Janus Publishers

Unit 1 Review

Name _____ Date _____

**A. Match each word on the left with its definition on the right.
Write the letter on the line.**

1. ears _____
2. body _____
3. subway _____
4. breathe _____
5. saliva _____
6. travel _____
7. dishwasher _____
8. skin _____
9. airplane _____
10. teeth _____

a. a vehicle with wings
b. hard white parts of the mouth
c. the outer covering of a person; flesh
d. clear liquid in the mouth
e. the organs by which we hear
f. a train that runs under the streets of a city
g. a machine for cleaning dishes
h. to take a trip
i. to move air in and out of the lungs
j. the physical structure of a person

**B. Find the word in each group that is not related to the other
words. Darken the circled letter beside that word.**

1. Ⓐ stomach
   Ⓑ intestine
   Ⓒ esophagus
   Ⓓ refrigerator

2. Ⓐ washer
   Ⓑ dryer
   Ⓒ sense
   Ⓓ dishwasher

3. Ⓐ subway
   Ⓑ motorcycle
   Ⓒ organ
   Ⓓ bicycle

4. Ⓐ taxi
   Ⓑ airplane
   Ⓒ esophagus
   Ⓓ ferry

5. Ⓐ toaster
   Ⓑ traffic
   Ⓒ oven
   Ⓓ stove

6. Ⓐ vegetable
   Ⓑ power
   Ⓒ energy
   Ⓓ electricity

Vocabulary: Meaning and Message © Fearon/Janus Publishers

Unit 1 Review

Name _____ Date _____

C. Darken the circled letter beside the word that is being described.

1. a device usually run by electricity that does a certain job
   - Ⓐ motorcycle
   - Ⓑ appliance
   - Ⓒ sense
   - Ⓓ digestive

2. a tube between the throat and the stomach through which food travels
   - Ⓐ intestine
   - Ⓑ esophagus
   - Ⓒ teeth
   - Ⓓ organ

3. a car whose driver you pay to take you somewhere
   - Ⓐ airplane
   - Ⓑ taxi
   - Ⓒ bicycle
   - Ⓓ motorcycle

4. meaning a great deal; having great value
   - Ⓐ muscles
   - Ⓑ breathe
   - Ⓒ skin
   - Ⓓ important

5. a vehicle with two wheels, a seat, handle-bars, and foot pedals used to turn the wheels
   - Ⓐ airplane
   - Ⓑ taxi
   - Ⓒ bicycle
   - Ⓓ subway

6. the part of the body that includes the fingers
   - Ⓐ ears
   - Ⓑ tongue
   - Ⓒ senses
   - Ⓓ hand

7. the organ by which we see
   - Ⓐ eyes
   - Ⓑ ears
   - Ⓒ breathe
   - Ⓓ taste

8. a kind of boat
   - Ⓐ transportation
   - Ⓑ taxi
   - Ⓒ vehicle
   - Ⓓ ferry

9. a vehicle with two wheels and an engine
   - Ⓐ taxi
   - Ⓑ motorcycle
   - Ⓒ subway
   - Ⓓ ferry

10. an appliance, box, or room for keeping food cold
    - Ⓐ oven
    - Ⓑ stove
    - Ⓒ refrigerator
    - Ⓓ dryer

11. a small room that goes up and down in a building
    - Ⓐ dishwasher
    - Ⓑ appliance
    - Ⓒ toaster
    - Ⓓ elevator

12. the opening through which food enters the body
    - Ⓐ skin
    - Ⓑ taste
    - Ⓒ mouth
    - Ⓓ organ

13. that which is heard
    - Ⓐ sound
    - Ⓑ touch
    - Ⓒ sight
    - Ⓓ loud

Reading on Your Own

Name _____ Date _____

As you read this story, think about the meaning of each highlighted word.

What Do You Like?

Some people like warm weather. Others prefer the cold. Which do you like best? If you like very, very cold **temperatures,** you might want to visit the Arctic. People live there year-round even though it can be as cold as –70 **degrees Fahrenheit.**

Few of us have ever known such cold weather. Degrees are units for measuring temperature. The temperature in the United States doesn't often go below zero degrees Fahrenheit. Fahrenheit is the temperature scale on which 32 degrees is the freezing point of water. The boiling point is 212 degrees.

If –70 degrees isn't cold enough for you, you might want to **experience** a day in Antarctica. No one lives there year-round. It's simply too cold. Scientists do stay there for short periods of time. The temperature on the **thermometer** doesn't often get above zero degrees Fahrenheit. The coldest temperature in the world was recorded in Antarctica. It was –128.6 degrees Fahrenheit. Without the right clothing, a person would freeze **solid.**

If you like snow, you might **consider** going to Sault Ste. Marie, Michigan. An average of 116 inches of snow falls there each year. If you prefer very warm temperatures, you might consider visiting Azizia in Northern Africa. On September 13, 1922, it was 136° F. The little circle after the number 136 means "degrees." The abbreviation "F" stands for "Fahrenheit."

If 136° F is too hot for you, you might think about going to Puerto Rico. The temperatures there range from about 70° F in January to 90° F in July. During the other 10 **months** of the year, the temperature doesn't **increase** too much or get much lower. In Puerto Rico, you can swim year-round.

If you like a lot of rain, you might want to take a trip to Mount Waialeale on the island of Kauai in Hawaii. From January to December, it rains about 460 inches. In other words, the **yearly** rainfall is almost 40 feet!

Do you prefer hot weather, cold weather, or a little bit of each? Why?

_____

_____

_____

Vocabulary: Meaning and Message © Fearon/Janus Publishers

Lesson 1, Exercise 2
Using Context

Name _____ Date _____

Use the words in the box to complete the sentences below.

experience temperatures solid degrees months Fahrenheit thermometer consider yearly increased

The coldest place on earth is Antarctica. The
_____ there are very low. In winter, they can
range from −40 to −80 degrees _____. It's so
cold in most of Antarctica that it doesn't rain. There is some snow.
But from January to December, the _____
rainfall is only about two inches. That makes Antarctica as dry
as a desert! In the summer _____, the
temperature gets a little warmer. But it never gets very much above
freezing.

At first, only a few scientists went to Antarctica. Now their
numbers have _____. These people
_____ the freezing weather first hand.

Antarctica is surrounded by miles of sea. Most of it is frozen
_____. It is very difficult for boats to move
through this dense ice.

If you were to spend some time in Antarctica, you wouldn't
need to look at a _____ to know it
was cold. Ten or fifteen _____
of temperature change probably wouldn't make
much difference to you. When you
_____ it, would −60° F
feel that much colder than −40° F?

South Pole

Pacific Ocean

Atlantic Ocean

Antarctica

Indian Ocean

Vocabulary Development: Synonyms

Name _____ Date _____

Synonyms are words that have the same or nearly the same meanings as other words. Synonyms can help you both in reading and writing. For example, suppose you are reading about the Arctic. The author might say something like this:

> For centuries, *frigid* temperatures kept people from reaching the North Pole. The *glacial* cold there could easily kill a person who wasn't wearing proper clothing.

"Frigid" and "glacial" are two ways of saying almost the same thing. The author makes his or her ideas more vivid by not using the same words over and over.
Suppose you read this:

> Many explorers *left* from Greenland to reach the North Pole. They *embarked* in all kinds of weather, including raging snowstorms.

Here you can tell that "embarked" means the same as "left." The author uses synonyms to make the writing more interesting.
You can use synonyms to make your own writing more interesting—that is, to make it more fascinating, exciting, amusing, or entertaining.
You can use synonyms to make your own writing more vivid—that is, to make it more intense, lifelike, distinct, or striking.

Vocabulary: Meaning and Message © Fearon/Janus Publishers

Lesson 1, Exercise 3
Vocabulary Development: Synonyms

Name _____ Date _____

A. Match the words in the left column with their synonyms in the right column.

1. increase _____   a. belly

2. yearly _____   b. every twelve months

3. consider _____   c. live through

4. experience _____   d. icebox

5. solid _____   e. devices

6. refrigerator _____   f. likely

7. appliances _____   g. become greater

8. travel _____   h. hard; firm

9. stomach _____   i. think over

10. probably _____   j. journey

B. Choose words from the box to replace the words in parentheses below. If you're not sure of a word's meaning, look it up in a dictionary.

---

a. balmy   b. consider   c. solid

d. scorching   e. icy   f. experience

---

1. Temperatures in the Arctic can reach a (warm) _____ 50° F.

2. Scientists in the Antarctic (live through) _____ the coldest temperatures on earth.

3. The (cold) _____ wind blew across the snow-covered mountains.

4. Sometimes the sun gets so (hot) _____ it burns the grass.

5. The extreme cold causes many people to (think over) _____ whether to visit the Arctic.

6. The ice is so (thick) _____ that heavy vehicles can be driven across it.

Puzzle

Name _____ Date _____

A. To solve this puzzle, choose a word from the box to fit each definition below. Write one letter in each blank.

Fahrenheit month thermometer yearly solid temperature consider experienced degree increase

1. to think over ◯_ _ _ _ _ _ _

2. measured during a twelve-month period _ _◯_ _ _

3. very hard _ _◯_ _

4. grow ◯_ _ _ _ _ _ _

5. a scale on which freezing is 32°◯_ _ _ _ _ _ _ _ _

6. a device that measures how hot or cold it is
_ _ _ _ _ _◯_ _ _ _

7. a number that tells how hot or cold it is _ _ _◯_ _

8. one of the twelve divisions of the year _ _◯_ _

9. live through _ _ _ _ _◯_ _ _ _

10. how hot or cold something is _ _ _ _ _ _ _◯_ _ _

B. Write the circled letters above in the order in which they appear. The letters spell a state in the United States. If you like outdoor sports, you might consider taking a trip there someday.

_____

Vocabulary: Meaning and Message © Fearon/Janus Publishers

Dictionary Skills: Guide Words

Name _____ Date _____

  As you learned earlier, the guide words at the top of a dictionary page can help you find words quickly. The guide word on the left tells you the first word defined on a page. The guide word on the right tells you the last word defined on a page.

  Let's say you're looking up the word *degree*. You might find these two words at the top of the page on which *degree* is defined: **defense** and **dejected.**

After each word are two sets of guide words. Circle the correct set of guide words for the word.

1.	**Fahrenheit**	fair/fall	factor/faint
2.	**temperature**	telescope/tent	terror/text
3.	**experience**	exist/export	exact/excess
4.	**increase**	indent/Indiana	incident/incubate
5.	**month**	moody/moreover	monorail/mood
6.	**solid**	sock/solar	sold/soloist
7.	**yearly**	yard/yesterday	yet/yolk
8.	**consider**	conserve/constant	convict/cope
9.	**thermometer**	theater/thesaurus	textbook/thaw
10.	**weather**	weary/wedge	wavy/weapon
11.	**Arctic**	arm/aroma	arch/argument
12.	**measure**	meantime/medallion	memorial/mention
13.	**scale**	scald/scarce	schedule/scoop
14.	**freezing**	Franklin/freedom	freeway/fret
15.	**boiling**	body/bolt	boom/border
16.	**period**	person/pest	perfect/perky
17.	**recorded**	recollect/recover	refuse/regular
18.	**abbreviation**	absent/abuse	abandon/about
19.	**Puerto Rico**	puddle/pulp	pulse/punish
20.	**rainfall**	rank/rash	railroad/ranch

Writing on Your Own

Name _____ Date _____

A. Imagine you have just been told you'll be moving to Alaska. Tell why you do or do not want to go there. Give three reasons.

_____

_____

_____

_____

_____

_____

B. Imagine that you see the following sign:

> **Win a Two-Week Trip Anywhere in the World!**
> **Just tell us where you want to go, and why.**
> **Winner to be announced soon.**

Enter the contest.

_____

_____

_____

_____

_____

_____

_____

_____

_____

_____

Vocabulary: Meaning and Message © Fearon/Janus Publishers

Lesson 1, Exercise 7
Test

Name _____ Date _____

Choose the best word to complete each sentence.

1. In deserts, there can be fewer than 2 inches of rainfall _____.

   A. yearly   B. increase   C. Fahrenheit   D. daily

2. We knew it was hot when the _____ reached 100° F.

   A. rainfall   B. degree   C. temperature   D. month

3. Thanksgiving comes in the _____ of November.

   A. day   B. yearly   C. century   D. month

4. I like to stay indoors when it gets colder than 10 _____ Fahrenheit.

   A. numbers   B. days   C. months   D. degrees

5. My aunt in Omaha asked me if I would _____ spending the summer there.

   A. consider   B. compare   C. explain   D. forgive

6. Crops can be ruined if there is a sharp _____ in the amount of rainfall.

   A. sound   B. degree   C. increase   D. month

7. A hot 95° F temperature showed on the _____.

   A. vehicle   B. thermometer   C. Celsius   D. experience

8. The coldest temperature ever recorded was –130° _____.

   A. Fahrenheit   B. degrees   C. hot   D. sweltering

9. Ice cubes are water that is frozen _____.

   A. lightly   B. heavily   C. in part   D. solid

10. Not many people have _____ temperatures as hot as 120° F.

   A. experienced   B. fought   C. allowed   D. proved

Reading on Your Own

Name _____ Date _____

As you read this story, think about the meaning of each highlighted word.

What's Cooking?

Bookstores have books on almost any **topic.** You can find books about sports and books about health. There are books on history, travel, and entertainment. There are mystery books and books of science fiction. In most bookstores, there are also a lot of books on cooking. It seems that everyone enjoys making a meal—at least once in a while.

Some **cookbooks** are on a single topic. The topic might be chocolate. It could be fruit. It could be breads. A single-topic cookbook includes many different **recipes**. But they all teach you to cook—or to cook with—that one main food.

One bread cookbook gives an excellent **recipe** for banana bread. It's easy to follow. The first step is to gather all the **ingredients**. They are: 1/2 cup sugar, 3 tablespoons oil, 1 teaspoon vanilla, 1/2 teaspoon salt, 2 cups flour, 1/2 teaspoon baking soda, 2 teaspoons baking powder, and 2 cups mashed ripe bananas.

Mix the sugar, oil, vanilla, and salt together. A fork is good to use for this. When these items are well **blended**, add the mashed bananas. In another bowl, mix the flour, baking powder, and baking soda. Then combine the items in the two bowls. Finally, spoon everything into a buttered pan.

Bake the bread for a **minimum** of an hour. You may want to leave it in the oven for an hour and a half. But a word of **caution:** two hours is the **maximum** amount of time. If you leave the bread in the oven any longer, it will be dried out. It also may be burned.

Not everyone uses a cookbook when making meals. Many people know the recipes for their favorite dishes. For example, many people like to eat pancakes for **breakfast**. They probably don't look up pancake recipes every morning. Some people often eat fish for **dinner.** They probably know many excellent fish recipes.

Cookbooks are helpful. But your friends and family can be even more helpful. They may have recipes they'll share with you. In fact, you might want to collect these recipes and make a cookbook of your own.

Describe your favorite meal.

_____

_____

_____

_____

Vocabulary: Meaning and Message © Fearon/Janus Publishers

Lesson 2, Exercise 2
Using Context

Name _____ Date _____

Choose a word from the box to replace the highlighted word or words in each sentence.

ingredients	blend	recipe	dinner	minimum
breakfast	cookbook	topic	caution	maximum

1. The sugar and butter were hard to **mix together well** because the butter was so cold. _____

2. I tried to follow the **list of food items and directions for making something to eat** for peach pie. But I used too much flour. The crust came out tasting like cardboard.

   _____

3. At around 6:00 in the evening, many people eat **the main meal of the day**. _____

4. There's a great recipe for paella in my Spanish **book that has information about food**. Paella is made with rice and chicken or fish. It's spiced with saffron. _____

5. We ate eggs and muffins for **the first meal of the day**.

   _____

6. The **greatest** amount of time I can spend with you today is two hours. _____

7. Some people are lazy. They spend the **least** amount of time exercising. _____

8. The sign gave pregnant women some words of **warning** about drinking alcohol. _____

9. Flour and water are two important **items that go into making a food dish** in bread. _____

10. I would like to know more about the **subject** of meatless cooking. _____

Vocabulary Development: Homonyms

Name _____ Date _____

A **homonym** is a word that sounds the same as another word. But it has a different meaning. And usually it is spelled differently. The words *whole* and *hole* are homonyms. The first word means "complete" or "having all its parts." The second word means "an opening in the ground."

It's important to know the different meanings of homonyms. Otherwise, you may misunderstand what someone is saying. Or you may be misunderstood yourself. For example, imagine telling your brother, "The tale is long and frightening." He thinks you're talking about the *tail* of the crocodile that you saw at the zoo. He asks you if the head is frightening, too. But what you're talking about is the *tale*, or story, that you heard at the zoo.

When you use homonyms in your writing, be sure to spell them correctly.

Many words in the story on page 46 are homonyms. Some of them are listed here. Use each word in a sentence of your own. If you don't know the meaning of a word, look it up in a dictionary.

1. **there** _____

   _____

   their _____

   _____

2. **main** _____

   _____

   mane _____

   _____

3. **two** _____

   _____

   to _____

   _____

   too _____

   _____

Vocabulary: Meaning and Message © Fearon/Janus Publishers

Vocabulary Development: Homonyms

Name _____ Date _____

4. **one** _____

_____

   won _____

_____

5. **for** _____

_____

   four _____

_____

6. **need** _____

_____

   knead _____

_____

7. **flour** _____

_____

   flower _____

_____

8. **hour** _____

_____

   our _____

_____

9. **know** _____

_____

   no _____

_____

Vocabulary: Meaning and Message © Fearon/Janus Publishers

Puzzle

Name _____ Date _____

**Each sentence below has one highlighted nonsense word.
Rearrange the letters to make a word that fits the sentence.**

1. If you **dlenb** ice cream and milk, you'll get a milkshake.

   _____

2. The **mmmuixa** temperature this oven reaches is 550° Fahrenheit.

   _____

3. I would like to find a cookbook on the **ptoic** of fresh fruit
   desserts.

   _____

4. "Stay away from the hot stove!" Oliver **atoecuind** his little sister.

   _____

5. We wanted to learn how to make tortillas, so we bought a
   Mexican **obokocok**.

   _____

6. It usually takes me an hour to make dinner. Sometimes it takes
   less time. The **mmnmuii** amount of time is half an hour.

   _____

7. Let's get up early enough to eat **satkrebaf** before we leave for
   work.

   _____

8. This cookie recipe doesn't have enough chocolate chips listed
   in the **redginsetin**.

   _____

9. If this afternoon's game lasts a long time, I may be late for
   nernid.

   _____

10. I've never made this kind of sauce before. Do you have a good
    pecire for it?

    _____

Vocabulary: Meaning and Message © Fearon/Janus Publishers

Dictionary Skills: Syllables

Name _____ Date _____

Dictionaries give you a lot of information about words. They tell you how to pronounce them. They tell you the words' parts of speech. They give you all the definitions of words. They tell you where words come from.

Dictionaries also tell you how to break words into **syllables.** A syllable is a word part with a single sound. For example, the word *book* has one syllable. The word *dinner* has two syllables: *din* and *ner.* The word *minimum* has three syllables: *min i mum.* The word *ingredient* has four syllables: *in gre di ent.* The **boldfaced** dictionary entry for each word shows how it is broken into syllables.

Knowing how to break a word into syllables will help you to pronounce the word correctly.

Use a dictionary to find out how each word below is broken into syllables. On the first line, write the number of syllables in that word. On the second line, write out the word's syllables. The first one is done as an example.

1. maximum ___3___ _____ max i mum _____

2. blend _____ _____

3. caution _____ _____

4. teaspoon _____ _____

5. tablespoon _____ _____

6. breakfast _____ _____

7. cookbook _____ _____

8. topic _____ _____

9. banana _____ _____

10. recipe _____ _____

11. pancakes _____ _____

12. excellent _____ _____

Writing on Your Own

Name _____ Date _____

Think of someone you would like to invite to a meal at your house. Write down the person's name. Jot down the date and time you would like the person to arrive. Write some ideas about what you might serve.

_____

_____

_____

_____

Write a paragraph inviting a friend to join you for a meal. Tell the friend when to come and what to expect to eat. Use three or more of these words in your paragraph.

> blend   breakfast   maximum   topic   recipe
> dinner   cookbook   ingredients   caution   minimum

_____

_____

_____

_____

_____

Vocabulary: Meaning and Message © Fearon/Janus Publishers

Lesson 2, Exercise 7
Test

Name _____ Date _____

Choose the best word to complete each sentence.

1. The apple pie was so good that everyone asked for my _____.

   A. breakfast   B. topic   C. recipe   D. dinner

2. "Do not drink while driving!" is a sign of _____.

   A. ingredients   B. maximum   C. caution   D. breakfast

3. Weight loss is a _____ we often talk over in my house.

   A. topic   B. blended   C. maximum   D. breakfast

4. Some people don't need to look at a _____ to know how to make a meal.

   A. dinner   B. breakfast   C. cookbook   D. topic

5. Start your day off right with a good _____.

   A. dinner   B. ingredient   C. cookbook   D. breakfast

6. Six of us will be eating dinner tonight. What is the _____ amount of spaghetti we can cook in that pot?

   A. recipe   B. maximum   C. caution   D. blend

7. To make cookies, you need to _____ flour, sugar, and butter.

   A. ingredients   B. recipe   C. blend   D. minimize

8. Anything he cooks turns out well when he uses good _____.

   A. blends   B. ingredients   C. breakfasts   D. dinners

9. You'll wake up hungry if you don't eat _____ the night before.

   A. recipes   B. breakfast   C. ingredients   D. dinner

10. Since I can't cook, I spend a _____ amount of time in the kitchen.

    A. minimum   B. blend   C. recipe   D. cookbook

Vocabulary: Meaning and Message © Fearon/Janus Publishers

Reading on Your Own

Name _____ Date _____

As you read the story below, think about the meaning of each highlighted word.

Pay Now—Or Pay Later

Today you can often choose how to pay for what you want to buy. Most stores like to receive **payment** in cash. To pay in cash, you simply give the cashier money. In return, you receive the item you are buying.

Some people prefer to pay for goods by check. When writing out a check, you write the date, the store's name, and the cost of the item. Near the bottom of the check is a place for your **signature.** You must handwrite your name there. Once the store accepts your check, the goods are yours. Later, the store sends the check to your bank. The amount of money written on the check is then taken out of your **checking account.** Your checking account must always have enough money in it to cover the checks you write. If it runs too low, you must **deposit** more money into your account before writing more checks.

Another way to pay for goods is with a **credit card.** This is a small, flat piece of plastic that you give to the cashier. The cashier hands you back a piece of paper to sign, along with your credit card. When your signature has been O.K.'d, the goods are yours.

Some stores have their own credit cards. The stores give them to shoppers when the shoppers open **charge accounts.** A charge account is a business arrangement. It lets people pay for things after they have bought them.

Another way to pay for something is with a **layaway** plan. You give the store part of the money for an item. The item is put aside for you. Each month, you make a payment. The date by which you must pay what you have promised to pay is called the **due date.** When you have made the last payment, the item is yours.

Many people try to save money for future use. One way they do this is through **savings** accounts in banks. Each time they deposit or take money out of their accounts, they give the bank clerk their **bankbooks.** A bankbook is a record of the amount of money in a savings account.

In earlier times, people traded goods and services with each other. If this could be done today, it might make things a lot simpler!

What do you think is the best way to pay for things? Why?

_____

_____

_____

Vocabulary: Meaning and Message © Fearon/Janus Publishers

Using Context

Name _____ Date _____

Circle the correct word for each definition.

1. money given in return for goods or services

   signature   payment   layaway

2. a small plastic item that lets a person buy things now and pay for them later

   credit card   savings   deposit

3. a plan whereby something is held for the buyer until all the payments have been made

   due date   charge account   layaway

4. a person's name written by that person

   installment   payment   signature

5. money put into an account

   credit card   deposit   layaway

6. a record of the money put into and taken out of a person's savings account

   signature   credit card   bankbook

7. money kept for future use

   savings   charge account   signature

8. a business arrangement that lets a person buy things now and pay for them later

   deposit   charge account   due date

9. the day on which the last payment for an item is to be made

   due date   layaway   credit card

10. an account that lets a person write an order to a bank to pay money from that account

    savings   payment   checking

Vocabulary: Meaning and Message © Fearon/Janus Publishers

Vocabulary Development: Compound Words

Name _____ Date _____

Some words are formed by joining two or more words together. These are called **compound words.** Compound words can be written as one word. *Dishwasher, blackbird,* and *pancake* are all compound words that are made of two words written as one.

Some compound words are written as two or more words that have hyphens (-) between them. Some examples of this are *get-together, mother-in-law,* and *jack-o'-lantern.*

Other compound words are written with space between their parts. *Ice cream, hot dog,* and *lunch counter* are examples of this kind of compound word.

If you come across a word you don't know, look at it closely. It may be made of two or more words you *do* know. If it is, you use the two words to help you figure out the new word's meaning.

A. In your own words, write a definition for each of these compound words. Then use each word in a sentence. If you need help, look back at pages 54 and 55.

1. **bankbook** _____

   _____

   _____

2. **credit card** _____

   _____

   _____

3. **layaway** _____

   _____

   _____

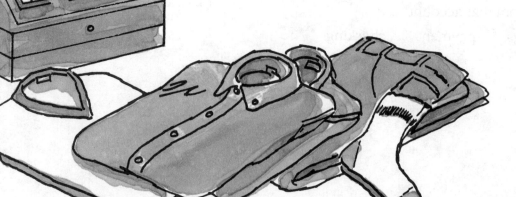

Vocabulary: Meaning and Message © Fearon/Janus Publishers

Vocabulary Development: Compound Words

Name _____ Date _____

4. **checking account** _____

_____

_____

5. **handwrite** _____

_____

_____

6. **due date** _____

_____

_____

B. Here are five more compound words. Try to figure out each
word's meaning without using a dictionary. Write your
guess on the blank line. Then look up the word and see if
you are right. Finally, write a sentence using each word
correctly.

1. **money belt** _____

_____

_____

2. **cash-and-carry** _____

_____

_____

3. **payday** _____

_____

_____

4. **checkbook** _____

_____

_____

Vocabulary: Meaning and Message © Fearon/Janus Publishers

Puzzle

Name _____ Date _____

Use the clues to help you complete the crossword puzzle. The answers can be found in the box.

| layaway | charge | payment | credit | signature |
| deposit | checking | bankbook | due date | savings |

Across

2. a plan in which a store holds an item until the customer has made full payment
3. an account with a store or business. It gives you a little time to pay for what you have bought.
4. to put money in a bank; also: the money itself
7. a person's name written in his or her handwriting
8. a kind of plastic card sometimes used when paying for goods

Down

1. money given in return for goods or services
3. a bank account from which you can take out money with checks
5. the date on which the last payment on an item must be made
6. a savings account record
7. bank account that you put money into for future use

Vocabulary: Meaning and Message © Fearon/Janus Publishers

Lesson 3, Exercise 5
Dictionary Skills: Syllables

Name _____ Date _____

As you learned earlier, a dictionary shows you how to divide a word into syllables.

Without using a dictionary, try to figure out how many syllables each word below has. It might help you to first say the word out loud. Write your guess on the first line. Then use a dictionary to find how many syllables each word has. Divide the word into its syllables on the second line. Finally, write the correct number of syllables for each word.

	How Many Syllables?	Words Divided into Syllables	Correct Number of Syllables
1. check	_____	_____	_____
2. deposit	_____	_____	_____
3. bankbook	_____	_____	_____
4. signature	_____	_____	_____
5. cash	_____	_____	_____
6. charge	_____	_____	_____
7. layaway	_____	_____	_____
8. account	_____	_____	_____
9. credit	_____	_____	_____
10. due	_____	_____	_____
11. payment	_____	_____	_____
12. cashier	_____	_____	_____
13. money	_____	_____	_____
14. store	_____	_____	_____
15. arrangement	_____	_____	_____

Name _____ Date _____

Imagine that you work in a department store. A young man asks you about the different ways to pay for a piece of clothing. Explain this to him.

First, list five to ten words that you think would be helpful in explaining the different ways to purchase goods.

_____

_____

_____

Now decide the order in which you will present the information. What will you discuss first, next, and so on? Put numbers next to the words above to show that order. If there are any more words you want to add, do so.

Now tell the young man how he can pay for the clothing. You may want to use some of the words in the box below. You will also want to use the words in your list above. If you need more room, use a separate sheet of paper.

layaway   payment   signature   due date
checking account   savings   bankbook
deposit   credit card   charge account

_____

_____

_____

_____

_____

_____

_____

Vocabulary: Meaning and Message © Fearon/Janus Publishers

Test

Name _____ Date _____

Choose the best word to complete each sentence.

1. Inez didn't like to take cash with her when she shopped. So she opened a _____ at her favorite store.

    A. deposit   B. layaway   C. payment   D. charge account

2. Kerry put $10.00 into her savings account. This amount of money was recorded in her _____.

    A. signature   B. bankbook   C. charge   D. savings account

3. Pema put away all the money she got for her birthday. Her _____ account grew quite a bit.

    A. charge   B. savings   C. payment   D. layaway

4. Lisa had only $4 left in her checking account. But she made a $50 _____ and then had $54 in the account.

    A. deposit   B. installment   C. layaway   D. credit card

5. Tina didn't take cash or checks with her when she shopped. She knew she could use her _____ to buy goods.

    A. signature   B. installment   C. layaway   D. credit card

6. The couch will be paid for on the December 1 _____.

    A. bankbook   B. credit card   C. due date   D. layaway

7. When you write your name, make your _____ clear.

    A. credit card   B. deposit   C. payment   D. signature

8. Jessica paid a small deposit on a new coat. She then paid $10 a month for the next six months on the _____ plan.

    A. payment   B. layaway   C. deposit   D. account

9. Donna just made the last _____ on her computer.

    A. signature   B. due date   C. payment   D. layaway

10. Quincy had $150 in his _____ account. After he wrote a check for $100, he had $50 left.

    A. checking   B. charge   C. due date   D. installment

Reading on Your Own

Name _____ Date _____

As you read this story, think about the meaning of each highlighted word.

A Place Called Home

Houses come in all shapes and sizes.

In early times, people lived in caves. There they were safe from wild animals and bad weather. Later, they began to build their homes with mud, grass, and bark. Still later, they built houses with stone and brick.

In today's cities, people often live close together. Many people live in tall apartment buildings. In some of these buildings, the rooms are quite small. The **length** of a bedroom might be 10 feet. The **width** might be 8 feet. That's only two feet wider than a tall person's height! However, in other apartment buildings, the rooms can be large. A living room might have 900 **square feet.** In other words, the length of the room could be 30 feet and the width 30 feet. You multiply the length by the width to get the number of square feet.

Some people live in houses on large pieces of land. The land might be in the shape of a square. In that case, all four sides would be of equal length. Or it could be in the shape of a **rectangle.** The opposite sides of a rectangle are of equal length.

In parts of Italy and Spain, houses are often built around unroofed central **areas.** All the rooms in a house open onto this space. In countries in the colder north, houses are sometimes tall and narrow. They have small windows to keep the heat inside. Newer houses built along a **coast** may have lots of glass so the people who live in them can look at the sea.

In some places, **similar** houses are built throughout an entire neighborhood. All the houses are made of the same material. They might all have the same number of rooms in the same places. The same type of trees might rise **vertically** from the **horizontal** ground. There may, however, be small differences among the houses. One driveway might be on the **opposite** side of a house from another.

Some people live in tents, others in log cabins, and still others in igloos. Whichever you like best, there's no place like home!

What kind of house would you most like to live in? Why?

_____

_____

_____

Vocabulary: Meaning and Message © Fearon/Janus Publishers

Using Context

Name _____ Date _____

Match the word on the left with its definition on the right.
Write the definition's letter on the line.

1. coast _____
2. similar _____
3. vertical _____
4. rectangle _____
5. area _____
6. width _____
7. length _____
8. horizontal _____
9. opposite _____
10. square feet _____

a. straight up and down
b. a shape whose opposite sides are of equal length
c. alike
d. how wide something is
e. seashore
f. flat, straight across, level
g. completely different
h. the total area in feet
i. how long something is
j. space, section, region

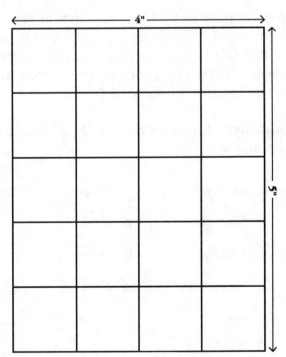

This rectangle is four inches wide by five inches long. In other words, its width is four inches, and its length is five inches.

To find the total area of this shape, multiply the length by the width. This rectangle's total area is 20 square inches.

Vocabulary: Meaning and Message © Fearon/Janus Publishers

Vocabulary Development: Antonyms

Name _____ Date _____

Antonyms are words that have opposite meanings. *Black* and *white* are antonyms. *Sad* and *happy* are antonyms. *Hot* and *cold* are antonyms. Antonyms can be found in many dictionaries. They come after a list and explanation of synonyms for the word. Here are the synonyms and antonyms for the word *hide*. The abbreviation *SYN.* stands for "synonyms." The abbreviation *ANT.* stands for "antonyms."

SYN.—**hide,** usually refers to putting something where it can't be seen; **conceal,** similar to **hide** but includes the idea of intent; **secrete** and **cache** refer to hiding carefully—*ANT.* **reveal, expose, make visible.**

Antonyms can also be found in a special book called a *thesaurus*. A thesaurus gives the synonyms and antonyms for words, but not their definitions. To find an antonym in a thesaurus, look up the word. Both synonyms and antonyms appear after the word. For example, the entry for *small* might look like this:

SYN. little, tiny, short
ANT. large, big, gigantic

Knowing the exact meanings of words will help you use them properly. And knowing the words' opposites will help you understand the words themselves. For example, the opposite of *sad* is *happy*, not *overjoyed*. If you know this, you also know that *sad* doesn't mean quite the same as *deeply depressed*.

A. Choose an antonym for each word below. Circle the letter beside the antonym.

1. **width**   a. narrow   b. length   c. area

2. **similar**   a. different   b. kind   c. open

3. **coastal**   a. wet   b. cheap   c. inland

4. **vertical**   a. horizontal   b. careless   c. failure

5. **opposite**   a. equal   b. same   c. width

Vocabulary Development: Antonyms

Name _____ Date _____

B. Each word below appeared in the story on page 62. Write an antonym for each word. Use your antonym in a sentence of your own. If you need help, use a dictionary or thesaurus.

1. **close** _____

   _____

   _____

2. **inside** _____

   _____

   _____

3. **tall** _____

   _____

   _____

4. **colder** _____

   _____

   _____

5. **narrow** _____

   _____

   _____

Vocabulary: Meaning and Message © Fearon/Janus Publishers

Lesson 4, Exercise 4
Puzzle

Name _____ Date _____

The words in the box can be found in the puzzle below. They may be written from right to left, left to right, top to bottom, or bottom to top. Find and circle each one. You may want to check off each word in the box after you have circled it. One word has been circled and checked as an example.

coast	similar	width	length	rectangle
✓area	opposite	horizontal	vertical	square feet

```
h o r i z o n t a l d d p r s t u v
s d t t t (a r e a) p d c r s q t u l
h s r e e u e r r e t a r i i t e e
d t d d r c p l d s s t r m i p l n
n n t d e r a a d a a l m i l a r g
h t d i w r c c i m c l t l p s t t
a v c d d r i i t c d w a a r d t h
v e r c n t c t l c r s i r t p r d
d e f g h e e r c o a s t e r t h e
f v e t t e v e t i s o p p o e r r
b c d e e f e v e l g n a t c e r i
r e f s q u a r e f e e t m n o p r
```

Vocabulary: Meaning and Message © Fearon/Janus Publishers

Dictionary Skills: Accented Syllables

Name _____ Date _____

A dictionary will show you how to divide a word into its syllables. It will also show you which of those syllables to pronounce more strongly than the others. It does this with accent marks. The accent marks tell you which syllables to stress.

A word with two or more syllables has an accent mark (′) over one syllable. The accent mark tells you to pronounce that syllable with a bit more strength. Here are some examples:

o′ pen   en tire′   wi′ der   in side′   a cross′   en′ try

Words that have three or more syllables may have two accents. One is a strong accent (′) . The other is a weak accent (′). The three-syllable word *rectangle* has two accents: rec′ tan′ gle. This tells you to pronounce the first syllable the loudest, the middle syllable the next loudest, and the last syllable the least loud.

Some words that have three or more syllables have only one accent mark. The word *similar* is an example of this: sim′ i lar. Here, the first syllable is the strongest. The second and third syllables are pronounced with equal strength.

A. Each word below has been divided into syllables. On the blank line, write the syllable that should be pronounced most strongly. If you need help, turn to your dictionary and study the word's accent marks.

1. **accent**   ac cent   _____

2. **pronounce**   pro nounce   _____

3. **vertical**   ver ti cal   _____

4. **horizon**   ho ri zon   _____

B. Look up these words in a dictionary. Each has two accented syllables. Write the word's strongest syllable on the first line. Write its next strongest syllable on the second line.

1. **dictionary**   dic tion ar y   _____   _____

2. **horizontal**   hor i zon tal   _____   _____

3. **multiply**   mul ti ply   _____   _____

Writing on Your Own

Name _____ Date _____

Would you like or dislike living in an apartment building? Tell why? Give three or more reasons.

_____

_____

_____

_____

_____

Suppose you are trying to sell a very large house on a big piece of land. What might you say to get someone to buy the house and land? Use details.

_____

_____

_____

_____

_____

_____

_____

_____

_____

_____

_____

_____

Lesson 4, Exercise 7
Test

Name _____   Date _____

Choose the best word to complete each sentence.

1. The ceiling is held up by _____ beams bolted to the floor.

   A. horizontal   B. vertical   C. opposite   D. coast

2. Susie's and Stan's houses look alike. The difference is that Susie's kitchen is on the _____ side of the house from Stan's.

   A. similar   B. horizontal   C. opposite   D. coast

3. Draw a _____ line across the paper from left to right.

   A. rectangle   B. square foot   C. vertical   D. horizontal

4. We need 150 _____ of carpet to cover the floor.

   A. rectangle   B. similar   C. square feet   D. areas

5. There is a small dining _____ beside the kitchen.

   A. vertical   B. area   C. coast   D. length

6. Bob bought Jack a tie for his birthday. The box was in the shape of a _____.

   A. length   B. width   C. area   D. rectangle

7. One hundred yards is the _____ of a football field.

   A. area   B. residence   C. success   D. length

8. The twins look so _____ that I can't tell them apart.

   A. similar   B. success   C. residence   D. exit

9. The beach along the Florida _____ is very beautiful.

   A. square feet   B. coast   C. width   D. exit

10. Two people cannot walk next to each other on that staircase. It's _____ is only 22 inches.

    A. rectangle   B. square feet   C. width   D. coast

Unit 2 Review

Name _____ Date _____

A. Find the word in each group that is not related to the other words. Darken the circled letter beside that word.

1. (A) credit
   (B) savings
   (C) bankbook
   (D) solid

2. (A) experience
   (B) cash
   (C) checking
   (D) credit card

3. (A) recipe
   (B) ingredients
   (C) yearly
   (D) cookbook

4. (A) consider
   (B) degrees
   (C) temperature
   (D) Fahrenheit

5. (A) month
   (B) year
   (C) increase
   (D) week

6. (A) credit card
   (B) layaway
   (C) caution
   (D) check

7. (A) deposit
   (B) ingredients
   (C) blend
   (D) cookbook

8. (A) length
   (B) maximum
   (C) width
   (D) square feet

9. (A) degrees
   (B) motorcycle
   (C) temperature
   (D) thermometer

10. (A) breakfast
    (B) mininum
    (C) meal
    (D) dinner

11. (A) savings
    (B) horizontal
    (C) deposit
    (D) bankbook

12. (A) area
    (B) width
    (C) due date
    (D) length

13. (A) recipe
    (B) cookbook
    (C) ingredients
    (D) signature

14. (A) rectangle
    (B) shop
    (C) cook
    (D) lunch

15. (A) tent
    (B) igloo
    (C) coast
    (D) house

16. (A) mouth
    (B) teeth
    (C) saliva
    (D) opposite

17. (A) airplane
    (B) subway
    (C) vertical
    (D) bicycle

18. (A) refrigerator
    (B) oven
    (C) dishwasher
    (D) charge account

19. (A) taste
    (B) payment
    (C) smell
    (D) sight

20. (A) similar
    (B) ears
    (C) mouth
    (D) eyes

21. (A) ferry
    (B) motorcycle
    (C) taxi
    (D) taste

22. (A) dryer
    (B) stove
    (C) floor
    (D) washer

23. (A) travel
    (B) transportation
    (C) vehicle
    (D) Fahrenheit

24. (A) esophagus
    (B) solid
    (C) stomach
    (D) intestine

25. (A) hear
    (B) breathe
    (C) smell
    (D) travel

Vocabulary: Meaning and Message © Fearon/Janus Publishers

Unit 2 Review

Name _____ Date _____

B. Find the word or phrase that has the same or nearly the same meaning as the boldfaced word. Darken the circled letter beside that word.

1. **maximum**
   - Ⓐ least
   - Ⓑ greatest
   - Ⓒ similar
   - Ⓓ different

2. **sounds**
   - Ⓐ senses
   - Ⓑ noises
   - Ⓒ birds
   - Ⓓ taste

3. **breathe**
   - Ⓐ listen
   - Ⓑ sound
   - Ⓒ take in air
   - Ⓓ esophagus

4. **refrigerator**
   - Ⓐ stove
   - Ⓑ kitchen
   - Ⓒ oven
   - Ⓓ icebox

5. **experience**
   - Ⓐ measure
   - Ⓑ live through
   - Ⓒ laugh at
   - Ⓓ leave alone

6. **increase**
   - Ⓐ grow smaller
   - Ⓑ enjoy
   - Ⓒ become larger
   - Ⓓ signature

7. **blend**
   - Ⓐ leave out
   - Ⓑ mix well
   - Ⓒ bake
   - Ⓓ eat

8. **topic**
   - Ⓐ cookbook
   - Ⓑ subject
   - Ⓒ ingredient
   - Ⓓ maximum

9. **minimum**
   - Ⓐ similar
   - Ⓑ most
   - Ⓒ least
   - Ⓓ blended

10. **caution**
    - Ⓐ warning
    - Ⓑ stove
    - Ⓒ bake
    - Ⓓ experience

11. **area**
    - Ⓐ rectangle
    - Ⓑ circle
    - Ⓒ square
    - Ⓓ space

12. **opposite**
    - Ⓐ same
    - Ⓑ likely
    - Ⓒ across from
    - Ⓓ similar

13. **similar**
    - Ⓐ alike
    - Ⓑ different
    - Ⓒ exact
    - Ⓓ big

Reading on Your Own

Name _____ Date _____

As you read this story, think about the meaning of each highlighted word.

Is It Right?

Think about this. Because he comes from another country, a boy isn't invited to a birthday party. Because of her sex, a girl isn't permitted to play a game of baseball. Because of his religion, a boy isn't asked to join a club. Because of her skin color, a girl isn't allowed to eat in a restaurant.

Discrimination is the unfair treatment of people whose backgrounds are different from others. People are sometimes discriminated against because of their race, sex, religion, or age. Discrimination denies people their **freedom**. It keeps them from choosing and acting freely. But people want **equality.** They want to be treated in the same fair way as others.

We can see many examples of discrimination in the world today. In **business,** for example, an **employer** might not hire a worker who was born in a foreign country. An **employee,** or worker, might not be given a raise because she's a woman. In housing, some people can't buy or rent homes because of their race. In **education,** some people cannot go to certain schools because of their religion, race, or sex. Discrimination affects everyone. It forces us to live our lives segregated, or separated from one another.

In the United States, there are now laws against almost all forms of segregation. On May 17, 1954, racial segregation in the public schools was ruled **unconstitutional.** It was against our country's Constitution, or basic set of laws, to keep children out of certain schools because of their race. On June 29, 1964, a civil rights bill was passed. It banned discrimination in such areas as voting and jobs, and in such places as hotels and train and bus stations. Laws, however, don't always change things as much as we might want them to. Some people continue to be **prejudiced.** Their thoughts, opinions, and feelings about others aren't based on facts.

We should all examine our **attitudes** toward others. The world would be a much more peaceful place if we treated everyone as they would like to be treated.

Have you or someone you know ever been discriminated against? If so, explain.

_____

_____

_____

Vocabulary: Meaning and Message © Fearon/Janus Publishers

Lesson 1, Exercise 2
Using Context

Name _____ Date _____

Choose a word from the box to complete each sentence.

a. business	d. unconstitutional	g. equality
b. freedom	e. prejudice	h. attitude
c. discriminate	f. education	

1. A Chinese proverb says, "By nature all people are alike, but by _____ widely different." It means that people are similar. But the kind of schooling they get has a strong effect on their lives.

2. The American writer Amiri Baraka wrote, "What does any man *want*? To be left alone with his life, and have some hope of making that life what he wants it to be." He was writing about the _____ to live as one wishes.

3. Charles Caleb Colton, an English writer, wrote: "We hate some persons because we do not know them; and we will not know them because we hate them." He is describing _____.

4. In the 4th century B.C., Aristotle said, "_____ consists in the same treatment of persons."

5. "If you look at the world one way," said the Irish writer Elizabeth Bowen, "there is always cause for alarm." She was saying the world looks either bright or gloomy depending on your _____.

6. In speaking about what to do with one's life, Horace Greeley said, "The best _____ you can go into you will find on your father's farm or in his workshop."

7. John F. Kennedy said, "Our Constitution is founded on the principle that all men are equal and citizens, and entitled to the same rights. . . ." It is _____, then, not to treat people equally.

8. Martin Luther King, Jr., said, "I have a dream that my four little children will one day live in a nation where they will not be judged by the color of their skin but by the content of their character." He hoped that people wouldn't _____ against others because of their race.

Vocabulary Development: Suffixes

Name _____ Date _____

A **suffix** is a group of letters added to the end of a word. The suffix changes the word's meaning. Look at each word in the left column. Read the suffix being added to it. Then read the new word.

Word	Suffix	Word with Suffix
like	-able	lik**able**
hope	-ful	hope**ful**
paint	-er	paint**er**

The word *likable* means "able to be liked." The word *hopeful* means "full of hope." The word *painter* means "a person who paints."

As you can see, some words change their spelling when a suffix is added. The word *like* becomes *likable* when the suffix *-able* is added.

Here are some commonly used suffixes and their meanings:

Suffix	Meaning	Sample Word
-able	able, fit for, worthy of	admirable
-ee	the receiver of an action;	appointee
	a person in a certain condition	standee
-er	doer, maker;	singer
	more	warmer
-dom	rank, fact, or state of	wisdom
-ity	state or condition of	insanity
-tion	act of, state of being	segregation

If you are admirable, you are worthy of being admired.

If you're an appointee, you have been appointed.

If you're a standee, you're a person who is standing.

If you're a singer, singing is what you do.

If it's warmer today than it was yesterday, it is more warm.

If you're looking for wisdom, perhaps you'll become wise.

If you worry about insanity, you're probably not insane.

If you've experienced segregation, you know what it feels like to be segregated.

Understanding suffixes can help you figure out the meaning of new words. For example, if you know that the suffix *-er* means "a doer" or "one who," you will know what *dancers, trainers,* and *swimmers* are.

Vocabulary: Meaning and Message © Fearon/Janus Publishers

Vocabulary Development: Suffixes

Name _____ Date _____

Combine each word with the suffix that follows it to form a
new word. Then use the new word in a sentence of your own.
If you aren't sure of a word's spelling or meaning, use a
dictionary or review the story on page 72.

1. **employ + er =** _____

   _____

   _____

2. **employ + ee =** _____

   _____

   _____

3. **employ + able =** _____

   _____

   _____

4. **equal + ity =** _____

   _____

   _____

5. **free + dom =** _____

   _____

   _____

6. **educate + tion =** _____

   _____

   _____

7. **discriminate + tion =** _____

   _____

   _____

8. **rent + er =** _____

   _____

   _____

Vocabulary: Meaning and Message © Fearon/Janus Publishers

Puzzle

Name _____ Date _____

A. To solve the puzzle, choose a word from the box to fit each definition below. Write one letter in each blank.

> prejudice discrimination freedom attitude unconstitutional
> employer education business employee equality

1. a person or business who pays others to work

   _ _ _ ◯ _ _ _

2. the condition of having the same rights and duties as others

   _ _ ◯ _ _ _ _ _

3. the state of being free _ _ ◯ _ _ _ _ _

4. not in keeping with the Constitution, or major laws, of a state or country

   _ _ _ _ _ ◯ _ _ _ _ _ _ _ _ _

5. the process of learning; gaining or developing knowledge or skill

   _ _ _ _ ◯ _ _ _ _ _

6. a person who works for another _ _ _ ◯ _ _ _ _

7. a judgment marked by fear and hatred

   _ _ _ _ _ _ _ ◯ _ _

8. the unfair difference in the treatment of people

   _ _ _ _ _ _ _ _ ◯ _ _ _ _ _

9. a way of acting, feeling, or thinking

   _ ◯ _ _ _ _ _ _

10. the work that people do, usually to make money

    _ _ ◯ _ _ _ _ _

B. Write the circled letters from above in the order in which they appear. They will complete this quote by John F. Kennedy, 35th President of the United States.

"All of us should have an equal opportunity to develop

_____."

Vocabulary: Meaning and Message © Fearon/Janus Publishers

Dictionary Skills: Pronunciation

Name _____ Date _____

A dictionary shows you how to pronounce words. It does this by using certain symbols. A pronunciation key explains the meanings of the symbols. In most dictionaries, this key can be found at the beginning of the book or at the bottom of each page. Here is an example of a pronunciation key:

at; **ā**te; tär; shâre; **end**; wē; **in**; īce; fîerce; **not**; sō; lông; **oil**; **our**; **up**; ūse; trüe; pu̇t; bûrn; **ch**ew; wi**ng**; **sh**oe; bo**th**; mo**th**er; **hw** in **wh**ich; **zh** in treasure; ə in **a**bout, ag**e**nt, penc**i**l, c**o**llect, foc**u**s

Let's say you don't know how to pronounce the word *freedom*. So you look it up in a dictionary. You see that *freedom* is divided into two syllables: free dom. The pronunciation spelling that follows this entry word looks like this: (frē′ dəm). The accent mark (′) over frē′ tells you to stress that first syllable. But how do you pronounce the ē?

Here's how to find out. Look in the pronunciation key to find an *e* with a short horizontal line over it. You will see that ē is pronounced like the *e* in *we*. When you say the word *freedom*, then, you know how to pronounce the *e*.

The pronunciation spelling of some words, such as *freedom*, includes an upside-down *e*. This symbol is called a *schwa* (pronounced shwah). The schwa is pronunced *uh*, as in the word *about*.

Write the correct word for each of these pronunciation spellings.

1. em ploi′ē   _____

2. prej′ ə dis   _____

3. ej′ ə ka′ shən   _____

4. biz′ nis   _____

5. em ploi′ ər   _____

6. i kwol′ i tē   _____

Vocabulary: Meaning and Message © Fearon/Janus Publishers

Lesson 1, Exercise 6
Writing on Your Own

Name _____ Date _____

Imagine that you've been discriminated against. You decide to write a letter to your local newspaper explaining what has happened. Here's what to do.

Think of an example of discrimination that *could* occur to you. Discrimination can occur because of race, religion, age, sex, nationality, and for other reasons. Write a few ideas about how you could have been discriminated against.

_____

_____

_____

_____

Now write a first draft of your letter. Begin by telling what has happened. Explain what you would like to see done. Then write a final draft of your letter on a separate sheet of paper.

Dear Editor:

_____

_____

_____

_____

_____

_____

_____

_____

_____

_____

_____

Vocabulary: Meaning and Message © Fearon/Janus Publishers

Lesson 1, Exercise 7
Test

Name _____ Date _____

Choose the best word to complete each sentence.

1. It's important to stay in school and get a good _____.

   A. assignment   B. attitude   C. education   D. respect

2. Ed's mother runs her own jewelry _____.

   A. education   B. business   C. employer   D. employee

3. The workers asked their _____ for more money.

   A. employer   B. employee   C. equal   D. constitution

4. To deny a person the right to vote is _____.

   A. business   B. equal   C. respect   D. unconstitutional

5. Each _____ in this office will receive a computer.

   A. discrimination   B. freedom   C. voters   D. employee

6. The Constitution says that all people must be treated with _____.

   A. equality   B. prejudice   C. discrimination   D. attitude

7. To keep people from doing what they want to do because of their race is to _____.

   A. business   B. educate   C. discriminate   D. independent

8. Stephen was sick, but he still had a cheerful _____.

   A. assignment   B. equality   C. attitude   D. employee

9. Because of _____, some employers won't hire workers whose backgrounds are different from theirs.

   A. education   B. equality   C. prejudice   D. freedom

10. Throughout history, slaves have fought for their _____.

   A. prejudice   B. employer   C. business   D. freedom

Vocabulary: Meaning and Message © Fearon/Janus Publishers

Reading on Your Own

Name _____ Date _____

As you read this story, think about the meaning of each highlighted word.

Guilty or Innocent?

Only one United States president has ever been **impeached,** or officially accused of committing crimes. After impeachment, a **trial** determines the person's guilt or innocence.

Andrew Johnson was the 17th president of the United States. He was impeached when he removed his Secretary of War from office without telling the Senate. Doing this was against the law. So the House of Representatives impeached him. Johnson later had a trial, but he was found not guilty.

In more recent times, Richard M. Nixon, the 37th president, was almost impeached. A serious **scandal** surrounded his presidency. A burglary had taken place in the offices of the Democratic party. It was thought that the White House had been involved in the break-in. Nixon said that wasn't true. He said that nothing wrong, or **improper,** had been done by anyone connected with the White House.

Congress held an **investigation.** People wanted to find out the truth. The Supreme Court demanded that Nixon give up tapes he had made of conversations he'd had in the White House. The Court thought that the tapes would help in the investigation. Nothing on the tapes was considered **unimportant.** The court wanted to hear everything. But Nixon refused to give up the tapes.

Impeachment hearings against Nixon began on May 9, 1974. The hearing were televised. There was great **international** interest, as people all over the world watched and listened. Nixon was accused of **misusing** his power. He hadn't acted as the President of the United States should have.

Nixon finally released the tapes. They showed that he had known about and helped try to cover up what had happened. Doing these things is **illegal.** It is against the law.

Nixon resigned from office on August 9, 1974. He claimed that people had **misunderstood.** They didn't really know what had taken place.

Do you think a president should be brought to trial if wrongdoing is discovered? Why or why not?

_____

_____

_____

Vocabulary: Meaning and Message © Fearon/Janus Publishers

Name _____ Date _____

Circle the correct word for each definition.

1. the act of carefully looking into, or examining something

    misunderstand   international   investigation

2. an act that shocks people's sense of right and wrong and often leads to loss of respect

    unimportant   scandal   trial

3. an examination of the facts by a court to find out if someone has broken the law

    scandal   trial   misuse

4. of no special meaning, value, or interest

    unimportant   improper   international

5. of or between countries

    misunderstood   investigation   international

6. wrong; incorrect

    trial   improper   misuse

7. to use wrongly

    misunderstood   misuse   scandal

8. to accuse a government official of wrongdoing

    impeachment   international   improper

9. not lawful

    impeach   unimportant   illegal

10. to form an incorrect idea of something

    misuse   misunderstand   impeach

Vocabulary Development: Prefixes

Name _____ Date _____

A **prefix** is a group of letters added to the beginning of a word. By adding a prefix to a word, you change the word's meaning. For example, if you add the prefix *re-* to the word "do," you get a new word: *redo.* It means "to do again."

Here are some common prefixes and their meanings:

Prefix	Meaning	Sample Word
il-, in-, im-, ir-	not	illegal, inhuman, immodest, irregular
inter-	among, between	intergalactic
mis-	wrongly, not	misspell
un-	not	unkind

Knowing the meanings of prefixes will help you when you come across new words. Suppose you read the word *impolite.* If you know that the prefix *im-* means "not," you'll know that the word *impolite* means "not polite."

If you know that *anti-* means "against," you can figure out what words like *antiaircraft* and *antiwar* mean.

Let's say you read a word like *immovable.* You know the meanings of the prefix *im-* and the suffix *-able.* So you know that *immovable* means "not able to be moved."

A. Look at each prefix below. Think of one word that contains that prefix. Write the word. Then use the word in a sentence of your own. If you need help, use a dictionary or look back at the story on page 80.

1. **mis-** _____

_____

_____

2. **inter-** _____

_____

_____

3. **il-** _____

_____

_____

Vocabulary Development: Prefixes

Name _____ Date _____

4. im-_____

_____

_____

5. un-_____

_____

_____

B. Combine the prefix with the word below to form a new word. Write the word. Then write a brief definition of the word. Use a dictionary if you need help.

1. **mis + treat =** _____

_____

2. **inter + state =** _____

_____

3. **il + logical =** _____

_____

4. **im + mature =** _____

_____

5. **un + lucky =** _____

_____

6. **mis + place =** _____

_____

7. **un + necessary =** _____

_____

Puzzle

Name _____ Date _____

Unscramble the highlighted letters to form a word that makes sense in each sentence below. The words can be found in the box.

trials   impeached   misuse   international   misunderstand scandal   investigation   improper   unimportant   illegal

1. The Senate failed to convict President Johnson after the House **c h i m p e a e d** him.

   _____

2. We won't know what has happened until we've made a careful **v e s i n t i a g t i n o** of all the facts.

   _____

3. A judge and jury are present at most **i l t r a s** .

   _____

4. There was quite a **d a s c n l a** in our town when the police chief was accused of stealing money.

   _____

5. A detective looking for information believes that no clue is **p o i m u n r t a t n** .

   _____

6. To steal another person's car is **l e i l g l a** .

   _____

7. I hope you don't **m s u n s t n d i d e r a** what I'm trying to say.

   _____

8. Several countries met for an **n e n t o a i t r a i n l** conference.

   _____

9. That's a screwdriver, not a hammer. Don't **s u m i s e** your tools.

   _____

10. Acting rudely is an **i p r m o r e p** way to treat customers.

    _____

Vocabulary: Meaning and Message © Fearon/Janus Publishers

Lesson 2, Exercise 5
Dictionary Skills: Pronunciation

Name _____ Date _____

   In the pronunciation key on page 77, you saw this line (⁻) over
the vowels *a, e, i, o,* and *u*. That line is called a "long vowel sign." It
means that you take more time to pronounce the vowel. It also
means that that vowel is pronounced in the same way as you would
say the letter. An *ā* is pronounced like the *a* in *ate*. An *ē* is
pronounced like the *e* in *we*. An *ī* is pronounced like the *i* in *iron*.
An *ō* is pronounced like the *o* in *so*. The *ū* is pronounced like the *u*
in *unit*.

   The long vowel sign appears in the pronunciation spelling of
many words. So does the schwa. Remember that the schwa (ə) is
pronounced like the first syllable in *about* and the *o* in *freedom*.

**Write the correct word for each of these pronunciation
spellings.**

1. i lē′ gəl _____

2. in ves′ ti gā′ shən _____

3. im pēch′ _____

4. kōst _____

5. âr′ ē ə _____

6. sā′ vingz _____

7. pā′ mənt _____

8. res′ ə pē′ _____

9. īz _____

10. tāst _____

11. vē′ i kəl _____

12. ar′ plān′ _____

13. bī′ si kəl _____

14. di grēz′ _____

Vocabulary: Meaning and Message © Fearon/Janus Publishers

Name _____ Date _____

Imagine that you are the president of your school's student council. Your vice president has accused you of wrongdoing. To defend yourself, you will give a speech in front of the entire student body. First, write down some details about what you have been accused of doing.

_____

_____

_____

_____

Now jot down some ideas about why you couldn't have done these things.

_____

_____

_____

_____

Begin the first draft of your speech below. If you need more room, use another sheet of paper. Look over your draft for any spelling or grammar mistakes. Most importantly, make sure it says what you want it to. Correct your first draft. Then, on a fresh sheet of paper, write a final version. If possible, give your speech to your classmates. Let them vote on whether you are guilty or innocent.

_____

_____

_____

_____

_____

_____

_____

Vocabulary: Meaning and Message © Fearon/Janus Publishers

Lesson 2, Exercise 7
Test

Name _____ Date _____

Choose the best word to complete each sentence.

1. His good name could be ruined by a _____ .

   A. impeach   B. scandal   C. illegal   D. collapse

2. The child broke the toy because he _____ it.

   A. misused   B. mistook   C. misshaped   D. impeached

3. The police conducted an _____ of the crime.

   A. misuse   B. investigation   C. scandal   D. arrange

4. The accused was given a _____ and found not guilty.

   A. trial   B. scandal   C. misunderstanding   D. due date

5. It all matters. It all makes a difference. Nothing is _____.

   A. illegal   B. misused   C. unimportant   D. investigated

6. If you do something _____, you could go to jail.

   A. trial   B. unimportant   C. collapse   D. illegal

7. If you listen carefully to what I say, you won't _____ me.

   A. misuse   B. misunderstand   C. investigate   D. impeach

8. Many countries met for the _____ meeting on arms control.

   A. improper   B. illegal   C. international   D. scandal

9. Only one United States president has ever been _____.

   A. proper   B. impeached   C. legal   D. understood

10. Pushing ahead in line is _____ behavior.

    A. improper   B. trial   C. impeachable   D. collapse

Vocabulary: Meaning and Message © Fearon/Janus Publishers

Reading on Your Own

Name _____ Date _____

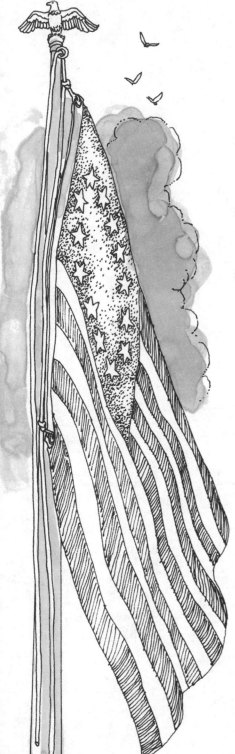

As you read this story, think about the meaning of each highlighted word.

A Two-Party System

Today, the Democrats and the Republicans form the two main **political parties** in the United States. Through these two groups, most people express their choices for president and for other government **officials.**

The Republican and Democratic parties didn't always exist. The two-party **system** began during George Washington's presidency. That was between 1789 and 1797. People disagreed about a number of issues then. One group, who called themselves the Federalist party, believed in a strong central **government.** Another **organized** group, the Republican party, held the opposite view. They thought the states should have more of the power.

The Republican Thomas Jefferson became president in 1801. The Federalists disappeared by 1812. But some Federalist ideas were carried on by the Whig Party. This party began during Andrew Jackson's presidency, which lasted from 1829 to 1837. The Whigs didn't agree with Jackson's followers, who were called Democrats. The Whigs later won two presidential **elections.**

In 1860, the Republican party elected Abraham Lincoln president. Since that time, the Republican and the Democratic parties have been the main political parties.

When one person or group holds all the power, there is no choice about who will rule. That type of government is called a **dictatorship.** In **democracies,** two or more parties exist. Voters choose their leaders. These officials **represent,** or speak for, the people who elect them. The officials are allowed to **appoint,** or decide on, other people to help them govern.

The two-party system has been in effect in the United States for almost 200 years.

What else would you like to know about the two-party system of government? Write your questions here.

_____

_____

_____

Vocabulary: Meaning and Message © Fearon/Janus Publishers

Lesson 3, Exercise 2
Using Context

Name _____ Date _____

Choose a word from the box to replace the highlighted words in each sentence.

> official government represents dictatorship election
> organized parties appointed democracies systems

1. Our senator **speaks for** the people of our state.
   _____

2. The governor is the highest elected **person who holds an office** in a state. _____

3. Throughout the world, there are many different **sets of laws or beliefs; methods** of government. _____

4. They held an **the act of choosing by voting** to decide who would take office. _____

5. In our school, the student **group of people who make rules** decides on the punishment for cheating.
   _____

6. The right to speak freely was taken away. A **government in which the people have no control** came into power.
   _____

7. The governor **selected for a position** two judges to the state court.
   _____

8. All the books in the library are **arranged** by subject.
   _____

9. In the United States, the two major **groups through which people express their political thoughts** are the Democrats and the Republicans.
   _____

10. Canada and the United States are two countries that are **governments whose power rests with the people**.
    _____

Vocabulary Development: Prefixes and Suffixes

Name _____ Date _____

In the last two lessons, you learned about prefixes and suffixes. As you recall, a **prefix** is a letter or letters added to the beginning of a word. A **suffix** is a letter or group of letters added to the end of a word.

The "internal spelling" of a word isn't changed when a prefix is added to it.

Prefix	Word	New Word
mis-	understand	misunderstand
un-	usual	unusual
re-	write	rewrite

Adding a suffix, however, *can* change a word's spelling.

Word	Suffix	New Word
admire	-able	admirable
happy	-er	happier
insane	-ity	insanity

Some words have both prefixes and suffixes. You can figure out the meaning of these words by knowing the meaning of the prefixes and suffixes. For example, if you add the prefix *un-* to the word *happy*, you get the new word *unhappy*. The prefix *un-* means *not*. So the word *unhappy* means "not happy." If you add the suffix *-ness* to the word *unhappy*, you get the new word *unhappiness*. The suffix *-ness* means "the quality or state of." So the word *unhappiness* is the state of being not happy.

Here are some common prefixes and suffixes. You learned a few of them in the last two lessons. Review them and study the new prefixes and suffixes.

Prefixes	Meaning	Example
mis-	badly, wrongly	mislead
re-	again, back	redo
un-	not	unlucky
dis-	not or opposite; lack of	disorderly

Suffixes	Meaning	Example
-ic, -atic	having to do with; caused by; dealing with	poetic, problematic
-tion, -ation	act of; state of being	education
-al	having to do with	musical
-ment	action, means, result; state of being	movement
-ship	state of	friendship

Vocabulary Development: Prefixes and Suffixes

Name _____ Date _____

Each word below includes a prefix and a suffix. Write the
prefix and suffix used in each word on the blank spaces that
follow the word. Then use the new word in a sentence of your
own. If you are unsure of a word's spelling or meaning, look it
up in a dictionary.

1. **undemocratic** _____ _____

_____

_____

2. **unsystematic** _____ _____

_____

_____

3. **reappointment** _____ _____

_____

_____

4. **misrepresentation** _____ _____

_____

_____

5. **reorganization** _____ _____

_____

_____

Puzzle

Name _____ Date _____

The prefixes, words, and suffixes below can be used to make new words. Read them and the definitions of the new words. Write the new words on the lines. Then circle the new words in the puzzle. The first one has been done for you as an example.

1. **mis represent ation**

    the act of representing wrongly _*misrepresentation*_____

2. **dis organized**

    not organized _____

3. **re appoint ment**

    the result of being appointed again _____

4. **un official**

    not official_____

5. **dictator ship**

    the state of having a dictator _____

6. **government al**

    having to do with government _____

```
d i c t a t o r s h i p c r w d r
n c l p u n o f f i c i a l r p i
p r i l w d c f r q u a i m e t u
a n r e a p p o i n t m e n t l c
w r m i c m r r d i s r e p r q r
a s c m i s g u i l t w u z r s t
r e c g o v e r n m e n t a l u v
d l c r i m t g h i j k l m n w x
m i s r e p r e s e n t a t i o n
a r d i s o r g a n i z e d i o r
```

Vocabulary: Meaning and Message © Fearon/Janus Publishers

Dictionary Skills: Multiple Meanings

Name _____ Date _____

As you know, a word can have more than one meaning. For example, people spread *jam* on their toast. They might get into a traffic *jam* on a highway. Some people try to *jam* into a concert hall to see a famous rock star. You might *jam* your finger in a drawer. You could *jam* on your brakes to avoid hitting a dog.

A dictionary lists all the meanings of a word. The meanings are numbered **1, 2, 3, 4.** and so on. The meaning that is used most often is numbered **1**. The second most commonly used meaning is numbered **2**.

Here are two meanings for the word *organize*:

> **organize 1.** to put things in an orderly way   **2.** to establish

Can you tell which definition of *organize* is used in each sentence below?

> The mayor will *organize* a summer work program for students.
> Today I will *organize* my files.

As you probably guessed, the first sentence uses definition **2**. The second sentence uses definition **1**.

Knowing a word's different meanings will help you to understand what is said and written.

Choose one of the words below. Underline that word. Then look it up in a dictionary. Write the first two definitions of the word. Then write one sentence using each definition.

    represent   **appoint**   **system**

first meaning: _____

_____

second meaning: _____

_____

first sentence: _____

_____

second sentence: _____

_____

Writing on Your Own

Name _____ Date _____

What qualities do you think the president of the United States should have?

_____

_____

_____

Why do you think those qualities are important?

_____

_____

_____

_____

What do you think is the president's most important job?

_____

_____

If you were president, what would you like to get done?

_____

_____

_____

_____

_____

Vocabulary: Meaning and Message © Fearon/Janus Publishers

Test

Name _____ Date _____

Choose the best word to complete each sentence.

1. Our class chose one person to _____ it at all school meetings.

   A. organize   B. represent   C. appoint   D. elect

2. The president of the United States _____ judges to sit on the
   Supreme Court.

   A. represents   B. impeaches   C. tolerates   D. appoints

3. Her sentences were _____ into a strong, clear
   paragraph.

   A. impeached   B. appointed   C. elected   D. organized

4. The form of government in which one person holds all power
   is a _____.

   A. dictatorship   B. democracy   C. election   D. system

5. In the United States, there is a presidential _____ every four
   years.

   A. political party   B. govern   C. election   D. dictate

6. The mayor is the highest elected _____ in the city.

   A. dictator   B. organization   C. official   D. government

7. No one can do it the way he does it. He has his own _____.

   A. elect   B. system   C. represent   D. democracy

8. The Republican _____ party won the last presidential
   election.

   A. political   B. dictator   C. appoint   D. govern

9. People with _____ jobs are supposed to serve the public.

   A. dictator   B. government   C. system   D. appoint

10. In a _____, you have the right to vote.

    A. democracy   B. dictate   C. system   D. appoint

Vocabulary: Meaning and Message © Fearon/Janus Publishers

Reading on Your Own

Name _____ Date _____

As you read this story, think about the meaning of each highlighted word.

Did the Pilgrims Eat Turkey on Thanksgiving?

Here's some information about United States history that you may not have heard before. Knowing it may not **affect** your life very strongly. But you may find it quite interesting.

The strongest earthquake in America didn't take place in the **recent** past. It happened on December 16, 1811, in Missouri. The state wasn't very built up then, and the damage wasn't great. The 1906 San Francisco earthquake was less strong, but it did more damage.

In 1913, the 16th Amendment gave the United States the right to tax its citizens. **Formerly,** there were no taxes.

The Pilgrims did not eat turkey at their first Thanksgiving dinner at Plymouth Rock. They ate duck, deer, goose, and seafood. The Pilgrims' neighbors, who'd taught them to survive in America, came to the celebration. It was the native Americans who'd made the Pilgrims' **presence** in this "new" land possible. The celebration included the retelling of many **incidents** that had happened since the Pilgrims' arrival. Everyone enjoyed hearing these stories.

The first strike in America took place in 1776. Listening to the **advice** of the leaders of their union, printers struck against their local shops. People strike when they feel they have been treated unjustly and when they believe in certain **principles.** These include the right to be paid fairly and to have safe work places.

President Gerald R. Ford, the 38th president of the United States, was born Leslie Lynch King, Jr. When he was two years old, his parents divorced. His mother remarried Gerald R. Ford, Sr. This man **adopted** the young Leslie and gave him his name.

The president cannot simply "push a button" to start a nuclear war. There are certain steps that must be gone through before this can happen. The president might even first contact both the country's **allies** and its enemies. The president's **conscience** would be clear only if he knew he was doing the right thing.

Of the facts listed above, which one surprised you most? Why?

_____

_____

_____

Vocabulary: Meaning and Message © Fearon/Janus Publishers

Using Context

Name _____ Date _____

Circle the correct word for each definition.

1. to take into one's family as one's own child; to make one's own

   advice   scandal   incident   adopt

2. ideas, information, or opinions given to help someone solve a problem

   conscience   incident   advice   principle

3. a knowledge of the difference between right and wrong

   ally   presence   conscience   affect

4. produce a change

   advice   affect   adopt   incident

5. having occurred not long ago

   recent   presence   affect   conscience

6. in an earlier time; in the past; once

   adopt   formerly   presence   incident

7. something that takes place; an event or occurrence

   ally   principle   presence   incident

8. a basic belief; a moral law; a rule of conduct

   ally   incident   conscience   principle

9. the fact of being in some place at some time

   presence   advice   effect   principle

10. a person, group, or country joined with another or others for a common purpose

    principle   formerly   ally   incident

Vocabulary Development: Confusing Words

Name _____ Date _____

Certain words in English sound similar to others, but they have different spellings and meanings. For example, the words *calendar* and *colander* sound similar. But they are spelled differently and have different meanings. A calendar is a chart that shows the days, weeks, and months of the year. A colander is a bowl-shaped kitchen tool. It is used to drain liquids.

There's little chance of being misunderstood when you speak words that sound the same. And if you are, the person you're talking to can ask you what you mean. But when you write, you need to know which word to use. Otherwise, there may be problems.

Imagine reading this note: "Please borrow a calendar from next door. We're having spaghetti tonight." You have no idea what a calendar and spaghetti have to do with each other. But you go ahead and borrow a calendar anyway. That night, you give the calendar to your brother, who is cooking spaghetti. Your brother thanks you for the gift. Then he asks, "Where's the colander?"

Here are several groups of words that confuse many people. Read the words and their definitions. Then use each word in a sentence of your own. If you need help, use a dictionary or look back at Lesson 1.

1. **affect**—to influence; to act on

_____

_____

    effect—result

_____

_____

2. **advice**—an opinion about how to solve a problem

_____

_____

    advise—to give an opinion

_____

_____

Vocabulary Development: Confusing Words

Name _____ Date _____

3. **recent**—occurring in the near past

_____

_____

    resent—to feel angry toward someone

_____

_____

4. **formerly**—once; in an earlier time

_____

_____

    formally—done in an official or proper manner

_____

_____

5. **principal**—most important

_____

_____

    principle—a rule of action; a basic truth, law, or belief

_____

_____

6. **presence**—the fact of being in some place at some time

_____

_____

    presents—gifts

_____

_____

Vocabulary: Meaning and Message © Fearon/Janus Publishers

Puzzle

Name _____ Date _____

Use the clues to help you complete the crossword puzzle. The answers can be found in the box.

formerly	incidents	ally	recent	principle
conscience	presence	adopt	affect	advise

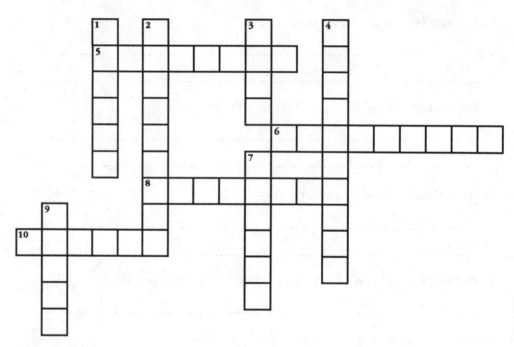

Down

1. to change; sounds like "effect"
2. rules of conduct; guideline; sounds like "principal"
3. friend; sounds like "alley"
4. sense of right and wrong; sounds like "conscious"
7. a little while ago; sounds like "resent"
9. to choose something and use it as your own; sounds like "adapt"

Across

5. before; sounds like "formally"
6. something that happens; sounds like "incidence"
8. existence; closeness; sounds like "presents"
10. instruction; guidance; sounds like "advice"

Vocabulary: Meaning and Message © Fearon/Janus Publishers

Lesson 4, Exercise 5
Dictionary Skills: Word Origins

Name _____ Date _____

Many words in the English language come from foreign languages. For example, the word *Nevada* comes from a Spanish word meaning "snowy." When Spanish explorers saw the snow-covered Sierra Nevada mountains, they gave the mountains this name. The state of *Nevada* later took its name from them.

A dictionary entry often includes the history, or *etymology*, of a word. This information may appear right after the pronunciation spelling. It may also appear at the end of the entry. Here is the etymology for the word *recent*:

Latin recēns, fresh, new

This tells you that the word *recent* came from the Latin word *recēns,* which means *fresh* or *new.*

Here is the history of the word *guitar:*

Spanish guitarra from Greek kithara, lute

This tells you that *guitar* comes from the Spanish word *guitarra.* *Guitarra* comes from the Greek word *kithara.* A kithara is a lute, a very old stringed musical instrument.

Knowing a word's etymology can help you figure out the meaning of an unfamiliar word. Let's say you know that the word *star* can be traced back to the German word *aster.* When you read the word *asteroid,* you can figure it has something to do with stars. An *asteroid* is a small starlike planet.

Choose the word that fits each explanation. Write the word on the line.

ally   **adopt**   **conscience**

1. It comes from the Latin word *alligare,* which means "to bind."

_____

2. It comes from the Latin word *adoptare,* which means "to choose for oneself."

_____

3. It comes from the Latin word *conscienta,* which means "moral sense."

_____

Writing on Your Own

Name _____ Date _____

Suppose you are going to give your classmates a short history lesson. You can describe any event in United States history. Jot down a few ideas about something you know about. If you can't think of anything, look back at the story. You can put one of those events into your own words.

_____

_____

_____

_____

Look over your notes. Decide which idea to present first, next, and so on. You can put numbers next to the ideas to show the order in which you will present them. Write a first draft of your lesson here.

_____

_____

_____

_____

_____

_____

_____

_____

When you finish your first draft, read it over. Make sure it says what you want it to. Correct any mistakes. Then write a final version on a fresh sheet of paper.

Vocabulary: Meaning and Message © Fearon/Janus Publishers

Lesson 4, Exercise 7
Test

Name _____ Date _____

Choose the best word to complete each sentence.

1. Their way of doing things is better than ours. We should _____ their method for ourselves.

   A. affect   B. adopt   C. ally   D. incident

2. The food you eat can _____ your health.

   A. advice   B. adopt   C. affect   D. ally

3. Newspapers report _____ events.

   A. adopted   B. principled   C. incident   D. recent

4. At a wedding, the bride's and groom's _____ is required.

   A. presence   B. advice   C. adoption   D. principle

5. During World War II, France and the United States fought on the same side. They were _____.

   A. allies   B. advisors   C. adoptees   D. principled

6. Jenna now plays piano in our band. She _____ played guitar.

   A. ally   B. formerly   C. advisedly   D. presently

7. "Do no harm" is a good _____ to live by.

   A. principle   B. incident   C. adoption   D. ally

8. My grandfather has many funny stories to tell. Each _____ he speaks of is more amusing than the last.

   A. ally   B. principle   C. lesson   D. incident

9. I shouldn't have done that. My _____ bothers me.

   A. allies   B. advice   C. incidents   D. conscience

10. She didn't tell me what I *had* to do. She offered me _____.

   A. advice   B. affect   C. presence   D. conscience

Unit 3 Review

Name _____ Date _____

A. Choose the word or phrase that is similar in meaning to the highlighted word. Darken the circled letter beside the word.

1. reliable **employee**
   - Ⓐ worker
   - Ⓑ dictator
   - Ⓒ business
   - Ⓓ attitude

2. fair **employer**
   - Ⓐ person who rules a country
   - Ⓑ person who hires others
   - Ⓒ government
   - Ⓓ political party

3. **misuse** badly
   - Ⓐ use incorrectly
   - Ⓑ adopt
   - Ⓒ organize
   - Ⓓ appoint

4. **international** meeting
   - Ⓐ political
   - Ⓑ having to do with more than one country
   - Ⓒ unconstitutional
   - Ⓓ illegal

5. **illegal** action
   - Ⓐ prejudiced
   - Ⓑ scandalous
   - Ⓒ not understood
   - Ⓓ unlawful

6. cheery **attitude**
   - Ⓐ education
   - Ⓑ outlook
   - Ⓒ system
   - Ⓓ election

7. **formerly** allowed
   - Ⓐ equally
   - Ⓑ in the past
   - Ⓒ unconstitutionally
   - Ⓓ improperly

8. helpful **advice**
   - Ⓐ suggestion
   - Ⓑ scandal
   - Ⓒ trial
   - Ⓓ investigation

9. **affect** our schools
   - Ⓐ bother one's conscience
   - Ⓑ appoint
   - Ⓒ represent
   - Ⓓ have an effect on

10. close **ally**
    - Ⓐ incident
    - Ⓑ principle
    - Ⓒ enemy
    - Ⓓ friend

11. **recent** development
    - Ⓐ official
    - Ⓑ new
    - Ⓒ old
    - Ⓓ principled

12. well-run **democracy**
    - Ⓐ dictatorship
    - Ⓑ government of the people
    - Ⓒ impeachment
    - Ⓓ investigation

13. **discrimination** because of race
    - Ⓐ politics
    - Ⓑ unfair treatment
    - Ⓒ attitude
    - Ⓓ equality

Vocabulary: Meaning and Message © Fearon/Janus Publishers

Unit 3 Review

Name _____ Date _____

B. Darken the circled letter beside the word that is being described.

1. one of the twelve parts of a year
   - Ⓐ yearly
   - Ⓑ degrees
   - Ⓒ month
   - Ⓓ organ

2. straight up and down
   - Ⓐ opposite
   - Ⓑ horizontal
   - Ⓒ rectangular
   - Ⓓ vertical

3. money given in return for goods or services
   - Ⓐ bankbook
   - Ⓑ payment
   - Ⓒ due date
   - Ⓓ layaway

4. a person's name written by that person
   - Ⓐ check
   - Ⓑ bankbook
   - Ⓒ signature
   - Ⓓ deposit

5. send an official to trial
   - Ⓐ elect
   - Ⓑ impeach
   - Ⓒ misuse
   - Ⓓ discriminate

6. of small concern
   - Ⓐ unimportant
   - Ⓑ official
   - Ⓒ illegal
   - Ⓓ improper

7. to put money in a bank
   - Ⓐ charge
   - Ⓑ check
   - Ⓒ date
   - Ⓓ deposit

8. the distance from one end of something to the other
   - Ⓐ square feet
   - Ⓑ length
   - Ⓒ similar
   - Ⓓ opposite

9. existence; life; being somewhere
   - Ⓐ misuse
   - Ⓑ education
   - Ⓒ presence
   - Ⓓ freedom

10. have the wrong idea about
    - Ⓐ impeach
    - Ⓑ misunderstand
    - Ⓒ experience
    - Ⓓ adopt

11. a small piece of plastic given by a store or bank that lets a person buy things at one time and pay at another
    - Ⓐ check
    - Ⓑ deposit
    - Ⓒ credit card
    - Ⓓ savings

12. an instrument used to measure temperature
    - Ⓐ thermometer
    - Ⓑ Fahrenheit
    - Ⓒ oven
    - Ⓓ degree

13. taking place once every twelve months
    - Ⓐ yearly
    - Ⓑ monthly
    - Ⓒ weekly
    - Ⓓ seasonal

14. schooling; training; experience
    - Ⓐ career
    - Ⓑ business
    - Ⓒ government
    - Ⓓ education

Reading on Your Own

Name _____ Date _____

As you read this story, think about the meaning of each highlighted word.

The Olympics

The Olympic games are international **athletic** contests. The games test, strength, speed, balance, and coordination. The **competition** is **fierce.** Everyone who enters them wants to win. Some of the events are track and field, gymnastics, boxing, swimming, basketball, and volleyball. The Olympic games are held every four years in a different city. The **anticipation** before the Olympics is great. People around the world look forward to the contests.

The oldest Olympic records date from 776 B.C. Those games were held in Greece on the plain of Olympia. The only event was the 200-yard footrace. The games were stopped in A.D. 394 by the Roman emperor Theodosius. Fifteen hundred years later, they began again. In 1896, nine countries participated in the first modern Olympics. A great deal of **cooperation** existed among the countries. Everyone worked together to be sure the Olympics would be a success.

Olympic **regulations** tell who can take part in the games and where they will be held. To **qualify** to enter the Olympics, you must be a citizen of the country you represent. You must sign a **statement** that you are an amateur. By doing so, you are saying that you don't get paid for being an athlete. You can be any age to enter.

Many people's **favorite** event is gymnastics. People love to watch the contestants balance on beams, swing on bars, and do spectacular tumbles. The athletes' **commitment** to their sports is total. They practice almost every day for years. They have to if they want to be called the world's best. All the athletes want to win gold medals.

The Olympic creed says, "The important thing in the Olympic Games is not winning but taking part. The essential thing in life is not conquering but fighting well."

Do you think all the athletes would agree?

Do you agree that the important thing in sports isn't winning but playing well? Explain.

_____

_____

_____

Vocabulary: Meaning and Message © Fearon/Janus Publishers

Lesson 1, Exercise 2
Using Context

Name _____ Date _____

Use the words in the box to complete the sentences below.

> athlete fierce commitments cooperate regulations
> favorite competition qualified statement anticipation

1. George Herbert wrote, "The lion is not so _____ as they paint him." He meant that a lion was not as violent as people said it was.

2. In 400 A.D., St. Jerome wrote, "No _____ is crowned but in the sweat of his brow." In other words, if you want to win at sports, you have to work hard.

3. James Boswell wrote in 1763, "That _____ subject, Myself." He liked writing about himself more than anything else.

4. Thomas Fuller wrote, "He is poor indeed that can promise nothing." Fuller was describing someone who can't make

   _____.

5. The Roman poet Ovid said, "A horse never runs so fast as when he has other horses to catch up and outpace." Ovid was talking about _____.

6. "Nothing is so good as it seems beforehand," said the English novelist George Eliot. She was talking about looking forward to something with _____.

7. Shakespeare wrote, "That which ordinary men are fit for, I am

   _____ in." He meant he was able to do what

   most people can do.

8. The French novelist Antoine de Saint-Exupéry wrote that when people work with others great things are born. In other words, when they _____, there's no limit to what they can do.

9. To keep law and order, many rules and _____ must be observed.

10. "A child should speak when spoken to," is a _____ mother often made.

Vocabulary Development: Suffixes

Name _____ Date _____

As you studied earlier, **suffixes** are letters that are added to the ends of words. By adding suffixes to words, you get new words with new meanings.

Here are some spelling rules to help you when writing words with suffixes. By learning them, you will be sure to spell these words correctly.

1. If a word ends in *e, drop the e before* a suffix that begins with *a vowel.* (Remember that the vowels are *a, e, i, o,* and *u.*)

   excuse + able = excusable; dance + er = dancer

2. If a word ends in *e, do not drop the e before* a suffix that begins with *a consonant.* (Remember that the consonants are all the letters of the alphabet except the vowels.)

   free + dom = freedom; state + ment = statement

3. For words that end in a consonant followed by a *y,* change the *y* to *i* before any suffix not beginning with *i.*

   happy + ness = happiness; merry + ment = merriment; prosper + ity = prosperity

Check your dictionary if you are unsure of a new word's spelling.

Combine each word with the suffix that follows it. Write the new word on the line. Then use the new word in a sentence of your own. If you are not sure of a word's spelling or meaning, use a dictionary or look back at page 106.

1. **fierce + ly =** _____

   _____

   _____

2. **athlete + ic =** _____

   _____

   _____

Vocabulary: Meaning and Message © Fearon/Janus Publishers

Vocabulary Development: Suffixes

Name _____ Date _____

3. **cooperate + tion =** _____

_____

_____

4. **believe + able =** _____

_____

_____

5. **regulate + ion =** _____

_____

_____

6. **carry + er =** _____

_____

_____

7. **state + ment =** _____

_____

_____

8. **anticipate + ion =** _____

_____

_____

9. **move + able =** _____

_____

_____

10. **merry + ly =** _____

_____

_____

Name _____ Date _____

The words in the box can be found in the puzzle below. They may be written from right to left, left to right, top to bottom, or bottom to top. Find and circle each one. You may want to check off each word in the box after you have circled it. One word has been circled and checked as an example.

anticipation   athletic   commitment   fierce   favorite
cooperation   regulations   qualify   statement   ✔competition

```
a b a n t i c i p a t i o n c g
t e s l g c o o p e r a t i o n
h f t c o m p e t i t i o n m m
l d a e p r e i q e e w q a m n
e c t v c r p q c c w r u b i t
t v e r o r b r i f c n a b t m
i h m c i r e d y y k l l y m n
c c e c t i i c o o u q i u e c
m n n x f z w t i r t y b i n o
g a t s d f g h e l k j y n t t
q z r e g u l a t i o n s k t o
```

Vocabulary: Meaning and Message © Fearon/Janus Publishers

Lesson 1, Exercise 5
Word Power: Nouns and Pronouns

Name _____ Date _____

All words can be placed into groups called parts of speech. A dictionary tells you which part of speech any word belongs to. The parts of speech are *nouns, pronouns, verbs, adjectives, adverbs, conjunctions,* and *prepositions.* Dictionaries usually abbreviate them.

noun—**n**	verb—**v**	conjunction—**conj**
pronoun—**pro**	adverb—**adv**	preposition—**prep**
adjective—**adj**	interjection—**interj**	

You will learn more about the parts of speech in the next three lessons.

Almost every sentence contains a noun or pronoun. As you learned earlier, nouns name persons, places, things, and ideas:

Persons: athlete, emperor, student, Anne Whitelaw
Places: Greece, Los Angeles, field, forest, school
Things: magazine, bridge, Golden Gate Bridge, contest
Ideas: truth, anticipation, cooperation, commitment

Pronouns are words that take the place of nouns. The most common pronouns are:

I, me, you, he, she, him, her, it, we, us, they, them

The words *anyone* and *everyone* are also pronouns.

Using pronouns allows you to avoid repeating the same nouns over and over. For instance, you could write the following:

Jane went to the store. She bought an apple and took the apple home.

But you could also write:

Jane went to the store. She bought an apple and took it home.

Underline the pronouns in these sentences.

1. I haven't seen you in years. How have you been?

2. Sue will be going to the store with Bill or me, but she won't be going with both of us.

3. We saw Karen and Pete yesterday, and they looked fine. Has something happened to them since then? What could it be?

4. If it happened to her, it could happen to him. In fact, it could happen to anyone. Everyone must be prepared.

Writing on Your Own

Name _____ Date _____

Imagine that one more person will be chosen to go to a camp that trains Olympic athletes. You would like to be that person. Write the sport you want to train in.

_____

Tell why you think you should be the person who gets to attend the camp. Include details about the kind of person you are. Tell why these qualities would help make you a good athlete.

_____

_____

_____

_____

_____

_____

_____

_____

_____

_____

Many people want to go to this camp. What is the one best reason you should be chosen?

_____

_____

_____

On a separate sheet of paper, write a letter to the camp director. Apply for the opening. Then read over your draft. Make sure it says what you want it to. Correct any mistakes. Then write a final version of your letter.

Vocabulary: Meaning and Message © Fearon/Janus Publishers

Lesson 1, Exercise 7
Test

Name _____ Date _____

Choose the best word to complete each sentence.

1. If you live in another city, you don't _____ to vote here.

   A. anticipate   B. regulate   C. cooperate   D. qualify

2. Before the winner is announced, there is great _____.

   A. commit   B. anticipation   C. cooperate   D. rule

3. "Ask not what your country can do for you; ask what you can do for your country." This _____ was made by John Kennedy.

   A. statement   B. commitment   C. competition   D. qualification

4. Why do we have to study the _____? Everyone knows what we can and cannot do.

   A. commit   B. compete   C. regulations   D. cooperate

5. When we saw how hard she worked every day, we knew how much _____ she had to getting the job done.

   A. commitment   B. anticipate   C. fierce   D. favor

6. We're going to have to learn to work well together. Our _____ will be important.

   A. statement   B. anticipate   C. regulate   D. cooperation

7. Although I enjoy watching basketball, gymnastics is my _____ Olympic event.

   A. favorite   B. fiercest   C. qualifying   D. athletic

8. All Olympic contestants have great _____ ability.

   A. regulating   B. athletic   C. anticipate   D. principled

9. Most soldiers fought until they died. The battle was _____.

   A. qualifying   B. cooperative   C. regulatory   D. fierce

10. Many people are trying hard to win. The _____ is intense.

   A. competition   B. regulations   C. statements   D. qualifications

Reading on Your Own

Name _____   Date _____

As you read this story, think about the meaning of each highlighted word.

Master of Ceremonies

Three "Top Ten" records came from his 1988 album *Let's Get It Started*. In 1990, he sold more albums than anyone else. He's a writer, a dancer, and a choreographer. He is also a producer and the head of a record company. Perhaps his greatest **achievement** is that he's the best-selling rap perfomer in history.

Born Stanley Kirk Burrell in 1963, he grew up in a rough part of Oakland, California. Many of his friends got into **trouble.** Ten of his friends from high school spent time in prison. Burrell was one of eight children. His parents divorced when he was five. At 11, he became a batboy for the Oakland A's. The players on the team called him "Hammer." They said that Burrell and the home-run champion "Hammerin' " Hank Aaron had a lot in common. Later, Hammer added "M.C." to his new name. The initials stood for "Master of Ceremonies." Still later, he dropped the initials.

Although Hammer tried to be a professional baseball player, he didn't succeed. But later, after two years in the Navy, Hammer formed his own record label, Bustin' Records. When his hit single "Ring 'Em" became a **tremendous** success, everyone began talking about this great new talent.

Hammer is **certainly** a very busy person. Aside from his music, he is involved in community work. He **especially** cares about young kids. And he puts his **beliefs** to work. He visits schools. He can be seen on TV talking about the effects of drugs. His *Please Hammer Don't Hurt 'Em, the Movie* shows the tragedy drugs can cause. Hammer gives money to programs that help kids in trouble.

Some people claim Hammer isn't a great musician. Others don't like the fact that he doesn't often write about politics. Most young people, however, would love to see one of his **performances.** The shows are thrilling. **Surrounded** by over 30 dancers, Hammer sings to sell-out crowds who **appreciate** his enormous talent.

What question would you most like to ask Hammer?

_____

_____

_____

Vocabulary: Meaning and Message © Fearon/Janus Publishers

Lesson 2, Exercise 2
Using Context

Name _____ Date _____

Circle the correct words to complete the sentences below.

1. My sister likes most rap musicians. But she _____ likes Hammer.

    especially   although   athletically

2. This evening at the theater, there will be a live _____.

    performance   achievement   belief

3. A friend of mine is in _____ and needs help.

    performances   trouble   achievements

4. Selling over 4 million copies of *Don't Hurt 'Em* is quite an _____.

    anticipation   album   achievement

5. Most people think Hammer is a great musician, _____ others disagree.

    although   thought   altogether

6. Hammer is often _____ by cheering fans.

    achieved   anticipated   surrounded

7. It's hard to have faith in others if you have little _____ in yourself.

    certainly   belief   performance

8. Thanks. I _____ what you've done for me.

    appreciate   achieve   believe

9. Everyone cheered loudly as the last song ended. The musicians were a _____ success.

    tiny   troubled   tremendous

10. If you go to tonight's concert, you will _____ see a good show. You can be sure of this.

    surrounding   appreciating   certainly

Vocabulary Development: Spelling

Name _____ Date _____

It's not always easy to know how to spell certain words correctly. That's because many words aren't spelled the way they sound. For example, some words include letters that are not pronounced. The word *ghost* has a silent *h*. The word *gnat* has a silent *g*. The word *wrong* has a silent *w*. The word *fight* has two silent letters, *g* and *h*. Many words end in a silent *e*, such as *wide, trade,* and *hole.*

Other words have letters that are pronounced in ways you might not expect. For example, in the word *photograph,* the letters *ph* sound like an *f.* In the word *especially,* the letters *ci* sound like *sh.* In the word *psychology,* the letters *psy* sound like *si.*

Often there are several different ways to spell certain sounds. For example, the word *so* has a "long" *o* sound. This sound can be spelled in several different ways:

grow   oh   toe   though   open   road

Although some words don't follow the normal spelling rules, most do. One useful rule concerns words with the letters *ei* and *ie.* Here's how to tell whether the *e* or the *i* comes first:

1. Write *ei* for any sound except the long *e.*

   w**ei**ght   n**ei**ghbor   th**ei**r   for**ei**gn

2. When the sound is a long *e,* as in *see,* use *ie* after any letter except *c.*

   f**ie**ld   bel**ie**f   th**ie**f   p**ie**ce   ch**ie**f

But there are exceptions to this. They include the words **ei**ther, n**ei**ther, w**ei**rd, and l**ei**sure.

3. When the long *e* sound follows the letter *c,* use *ei.*

   rec**ei**ve   c**ei**ling   rec**ei**pt

You may find it helpful to memorize words that aren't spelled the way they sound. Here are two steps to take to good spelling:

- Keep a list of words you often misspell. Practice saying these words aloud and writing them correctly.
- Use a dictionary whenever you're not sure how to spell a word.

Vocabulary: Meaning and Message © Fearon/Janus Publishers

Vocabulary Development: Spelling

Name _____ Date _____

Each word below is spelled four different ways, but only one is correct. Underline the correctly spelled word. Then write it on the line. If you need help, use a dictionary or look back at the story on page 114.

1. beleef   beleif   belief   belefe

   _____

2. acheevement   achievement   acheivement   achevement

   _____

3. trobel   truhble   trouble   troubel

   _____

4. although   althou   alltho   althuogh

   _____

5. certanely   certianley   sertanly   certainly

   _____

Puzzle

Name _____ Date _____

A. Choose a word from the box to complete each sentence below. Write one letter in each blank.

> performance surrounded trouble although beliefs
> achievement certainly appreciated especially

1. I have to watch my step and stay out of

   _ _ _ _ _ _ _.

2. To overcome those hardships was a great

   _ _ _ _ _ _ _ _ _ _ _.

3. I didn't get to that show. The tickets to every

   _ _ _○_ _ _○_ _ _ were sold out.

4. They were in front, in back, and on both sides of us. We were

   _ _ _ _ _○_ _ _.

5. We plan to go shopping, _ _○_ _ _ _ _ we don't have much money.

6. She○_ _ _ _ _ _ _ _ _○your gift.

7. I don't see things the way you do. We have different

   _ _ _○_ _ _.

8. After three performances, the musician must have

   ○_ _ _ _ _ _ _ been tired.

9. We liked everything about the concert,

   _ _ _ _ _ _ _ _ _ _ the dancers.

B. Put the circled letters above on the lines below to get a word that could describe Hammer.

_ _ _ _ _ _ _ _ _
              t

Vocabulary: Meaning and Message © Fearon/Janus Publishers

Lesson 2, Exercise 5
Word Power: Verbs

Name _____ Date _____

Nouns and **verbs** are the most frequently used parts of speech. Dictionaries usually abbreviate the word *verb* as *v*. Verbs are words that express action or state of being.

Action Verbs: run, talk, sing, dance, laugh, write

These verbs show *physical* action. *Mental* action is shown by verbs like these: think, imagine, wish, wonder

State-of-Being Verbs: is, are, was, were, am, will be

To show that something took place in the past, we use a verb's past tense. The past tense of most verbs is formed by adding *d* or *ed* to the verb:

Present Tense: walk   dance   laugh
Past Tense: walked   danced   laughed

Some verbs, however, aren't formed this way. For example, the past tense of *sing* is *sang*. The past tense of *run* is *ran*. We call these verbs **irregular** verbs.

A dictionary will give you the past tense of any verb.

A. Write the past tense of these verbs by adding *d* or *ed* to them.

1. achieve _____   3. perform _____

2. surround _____   4. appreciate _____

B. Use your dictionary to find the past tense of these irregular verbs.

1. write _____   6. grow _____

2. think _____   7. eat _____

3. sell _____   8. come _____

4. know _____   9. go _____

5. run _____   10. see _____

Writing on Your Own

Name _____ Date _____

Imagine that you review concerts for your school or local newspaper. Write your reactions to a concert you recently saw. Come up with a few ideas about a performer and a performance. Include the performer's name, the type of music he or she played, and when and where the concert was held. Also note what you liked and disliked about the music and the show.

_____

_____

_____

_____

Use your notes to write a first draft of your review below. Be sure to include the details you wrote above.

_____

_____

_____

_____

_____

_____

_____

_____

Go over what you've written to make it as clear as you can. Then write a final draft on a clean sheet of paper. You might want to read your review to your classmates to get their responses.

Vocabulary: Meaning and Message © Fearon/Janus Publishers

Lesson 2, Exercise 7
Test

Name _____ Date _____

Choose the best word to fit each definition.

1. a show meant to entertain an audience

   A. singer   B. crowd   C. performance   D. belief

2. a difficult or dangerous situation

   A. belief   B. trouble   C. perform   D. achievement

3. form a circle around

   A. surround   B. believe   C. achieve   D. appreciate

4. in spite of the fact that

   A. trouble   B. surrounded   C. although   D. certainly

5. something accomplished

   A. surround   B. anticipate   C. big   D. achievement

6. to be grateful for; to know the value of

   A. appreciate   B. believe   C. perform   D. achieve

7. surely; beyond a doubt

   A. anticipation   B. belief   C. trouble   D. certainly

8. an acceptance or trust that something is true

   A. certainly   B. belief   C. anticipation   D. perform

9. mainly; more than usual; to a great degree

   A. especially   B. trouble   C. although   D. often

10. enormous; very great

   A. fierce   B. success   C. achieve   D. tremendous

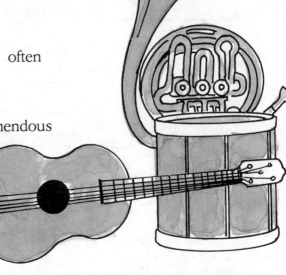

Vocabulary: Meaning and Message © Fearon/Janus Publishers

Unit 4: Sports and Entertainment   **121**

Reading on Your Own

Name _____ Date _____

As you read this story, think about the meaning of each highlighted word.

TV or Not TV?

In the 20th century, there have been many amazing inventions. The automobile, the airplane, the computer, and nuclear power have all changed our lives. But one invention has probably influenced us more than any of these.

Television is considered a most **incredible** invention. Watching it, you can see a person land on the moon, a war on the other side of the world, and a local school-board meeting. Television entertains us with game shows, sporting events, and soap operas. And it can be turned on 24 hours a day.

Although many people would say that television is a wonderful invention, others would **disagree**. Television doesn't please them. They are **dissatisfied** with it. They say television ruins family life because people don't take the time to talk to each other. It keeps people from reading books. It keeps them from getting up and exercising. Looking through a television **schedule,** some people find many of the programs **irrelevant.** They feel that the shows don't speak to people's real needs and desires.

In the United States today, almost every household has one television set. Televisions are **inexpensive** enough that some families can afford to own more than one set. Many people feel that this is really **unnecessary.** It just simply isn't needed. But there are also those who feel that everyone should have his or her own **individual** set.

The issues surrounding television aren't simple. In fact, they're quite **complicated.** As long as it exists, it's likely that people will have different opinions about television. It will probably remain a **controversial** subject.

What is your opinion about the value of television?

_____

_____

_____

Vocabulary: Meaning and Message © Fearon/Janus Publishers

Lesson 3, Exercise 2
Using Context

Name _____ Date _____

Circle the letter of the word or phrase that has the same or nearly the same meaning as the boldfaced word.

1. an **unnecessary** purchase

   A. not needed   B. hoped for   C. needed   D. wanted

2. a **dissatisfied** customer

   A. happy   B. fulfilled   C. angry   D. not content

3. an **incredible** story

   A. sad   B. complicated   C. amazing   D. true

4. an **irrelevant** detail

   A. historic   B. unimportant   C. true   D. important

5. a **controversial** subject

   A. open   B. proven   C. interesting   D. boring

6. to **disagree** with a friend

   A. organize   B. achieve   C. perform   D. argue

7. **inexpensive** jewelry

   A. costing a lot   B. not costly   C. shiny   D. fake

8. a busy **schedule**

   A. career   B. performance   C. list   D. evening

9. **individual** pizzas

   A. group   B. for one person   C. large   D. important

10. a **complicated** explanation

    A. easy   B. not simple   C. needed   D. short

Vocabulary: Meaning and Message © Fearon/Janus Publishers

Vocabulary Development: Analogies

Name _____ Date _____

Analogy questions appear on many tests. Analogies deal with relationships between words and pairs of words. An analogy test question includes two pairs of words. To answer the question, you must understand the relationship between the words in the first pair. This relationship will be the same as the one between the words in the second pair.

front is to **back** as **little** is to: A. tiny B. big C. middle

To answer this question, first figure out the relationship between *front* and *back*. They are opposites. So the second pair of words must also be opposites. What is the opposite of *little?* The answer is B, *big*. Here's another:

happy is to **joyful** as **cold** is to: A. hot B. warm C. freezing

What is the relationship between *happy* and *joyful?* They are synonyms, words that mean the same or nearly the same. To solve the analogy, find the synonym for *cold*. The answer is C, *freezing*.

Other relationships can be found in analogies. For example, one word might be a category or group that includes the other word, such as *month* and *day*. One word might describe the other word, such as *dry* and *desert*. One word can tell how the other one moves, such as *flies* and *airplane*.

A. Find the relationship between the first two words. Then find the same relationship between the third word and a word in the box. Write the word on the line.

incredible	irrelevant	disagree
inexpensive	schedule	individual	complicated

1. **throw** is to **toss** as **single** is to_____

2. **sad** is to **gloomy** as **list** is to _____

3. **black** is to **white** as **costly** is to_____

4. **end** is to **finish** as **differ** is to _____

5. **friend** is to **enemy** as **simple** is to _____

6. **beginning** is to **end** as **believable** is to _____

7. **necessary** is to **unnecessary** as **relevant** is to _____

Vocabulary: Meaning and Message © Fearon/Janus Publishers

Vocabulary Development: Analogies

Name _____ Date _____

B. Choose the best word to complete each analogy.

1. **tiny** is to **small** as **success** is to

   A. trouble   B. certainly   C. achievement   D. belief

2. **crawls** is to **baby** as **bakes** is to

   A. refrigerator   B. ferry   C. esophagus   D. oven

3. **appoint** is to **judge** as **elect** is to

   A. system   B. official   C. trial   D. impeach

4. **see** is to **eyes** as **hear** is to

   A. ears   B. mouth   C. skin   D. touch

5. **wings** is to **airplane** as **wheels** is to

   A. ferry   B. vehicle   C. transportation   D. bicycle

6. **cleans** is to **dishwasher** as **cools** is to

   A. elevator   B. refrigerator   C. subway   D. toaster

7. **inches** is to **ruler** as **degrees** is to

   A. thermometer   B. month   C. experience   D. solid

8. **hot** is to **cold** as **maximum** is to

   A. decrease   B. mouth   C. caution   D. minimum

9. **length** is to **width** as **horizontal** is to

   A. parallel   B. square feet   C. rectangle   D. vertical

10. **show** is to **performance** as **rule** is to

    A. beliefs   B. regulation   C. commitments   D. schedules

Vocabulary: Meaning and Message © Fearon/Janus Publishers

Puzzle

Name _____ Date _____

Unscramble the highlighted letters to form words that make sense in the sentences below. The correctly spelled words are in the box. Write the letters on the lines.

> **a. disagree d. unnecessary g. individual j. dissatisfied**
> **b. schedule e. incredible h. complicated**
> **c. inexpensive f. irrelevant i. controversial**

1. Just give me the facts. Don't include any **r a i v r e e l n t** information. _____

2. The story about the boy and the dragon was too **c r i b i n e d l e** to accept. _____

3. Today's , computers are **e x s v i n p e n i e** compared to the ones that were sold 20 years ago. _____

4. I can't see you this week. My **u l c s h e d e** is too crowded with things to do. _____

5. My parents and I often **a g d s i r e e** about which TV show to watch. _____

6. I arrived at Tom's house an hour late because the directions to get there were so **i c t p l c m o a e d**. _____

7. Politics and religion are **t r a l c o n i o s v e r** subjects. Many people express different opinions about them. _____

8. The computer didn't do what I hoped it would. I was **i s f e d s a t i i d s** and took it back to the store. _____

9. Driving me to the bus station is **s s y n n u e a r c e**. I enjoy walking _____.

10. The **i n a l d i d u v i** wish of each member is important to this group. _____

Vocabulary: Meaning and Message © Fearon/Janus Publishers

Word Power: Adjectives and Adverbs

Name _____ Date _____

Adjectives and adverbs are parts of speech.

An **adjective** is a word that describes a noun or a pronoun. In a dictionary, the word *adjective* is often abbreviated as *adj*. Adjectives are *important* words. Without them, a bike would simply be a bike, and not a *dented, rusty, black racing* bike or a *shiny, new yellow* bike. All these italicized words are adjectives. They describe the noun *bike*. They make it stand out in your mind. They tell you what the bike is like.

An **adverb** is a word that describes a verb, an adjective, or another adverb. Adverbs tell how, where, when, or how often something is done. In a dictionary, the word *adverb* is often abbreviated *adv*. Like adjectives, adverbs liven up your sentences. For example, you might write that you walked to school today. But, how did you walk? Was it *slowly, quickly, carefully,* or *sleepily?* Which adverb would you use to describe the verb *walked?*

A. Write a noun that can be described by each adjective.

1. controversial _____

2. unnecessary _____

3. dissatisfied _____

4. incredible _____

B. Underline the adverb in each sentence. Then use the adverb in a sentence of your own.

1. I've never heard anyone sing that loudly.

   _____

   _____

2. She wasn't there when I called.

   _____

   _____

3. Barbara finished the race first.

   _____

   _____

4. Bill always tells the truth.

   _____

   _____

Writing on Your Own

Name _____ Date _____

Imagine that your school is planning an experiment. For one week, none of the students will watch television. How do you feel about this? Is the experiment worth doing?
Write one sentence stating how you feel.

_____

_____

List reasons that support your point of view.

_____

_____

_____

_____

_____

Now list reasons that support the opposite point of view. Answer each of these reason's.

_____

_____

_____

_____

_____

_____

_____

_____

On a separate sheet of paper, write a first draft of your argument. Before writing a final version, make sure your argument is strong and clear. Add any new ideas you may have. Correct any errors.

Vocabulary: Meaning and Message © Fearon/Janus Publishers

Lesson 3, Exercise 7
Test

Name _____ Date _____

Choose the best word to complete each sentence.

1. Because he was in a rush and had a lot to say, his argument sounded _____.

   A. complicated   B. long   C. costly   D. short

2. We won't know when we're going to get there until we look at the train _____.

   A. controversy   B. schedule   C. expense   D. satisfy

3. We decided we had enough money to eat out when we found a very _____ restaurant.

   A. large   B. irrelevant   C. inexpensive   D. small

4. We have such different ideas about what we want. It's no wonder we _____ so much.

   A. complicate   B. dissatisfy   C. agree   D. disagree

5. It will take a while to hear everyone's ideas. This is a very _____ subject.

   A. satisfied   B. controversial   C. tall   D. nice

6. I don't know how you could have done so much so soon. I find it _____!

   A. necessary   B. expensive   C. mean   D. incredible

7. I heard that story yesterday. Hearing it again today would be _____.

   A. unnecessary   B. expensive   C. agree   D. satisfy

8. I suppose when you didn't get what you asked for you felt _____.

   A. short   B. tall   C. dissatisfied   D. happy

9. Tell me what's important, not what's _____.

   A. irrelevant   B. complicate   C. expensive   D. credible

10. The teacher listened to each _____ student.

    A. necessary   B. individual   C. credible   D. relevant

Reading on Your Own

Name _____ Date _____

As you read this story, think about the meaning of each highlighted word.

Take Me Out to the Ball Game!

Do you know which sport is **regarded** as the national game of the United States? It's baseball, and it's been played here for about 150 years. People disagree about the **origin** of the game. Some say it came from a British game called rounders. Others say baseball developed from cricket. But many people feel that the true origin of baseball is town ball. Town ball was played on New England village greens in the early 1800s.

The founder of baseball is also in question. For a long time, it was thought to be Abner Doubleday. He set up a diamond-shaped field in Cooperstown, New York, in 1839. In 1907, a group of people tried to find out the real history of the sport. When it **completed** its study, it said that Doubleday had invented baseball. But later **research** showed that this wasn't the case. Alexander Cartwright is considered by most **reliable** sources to be the founder of baseball as we know it today. In 1845, Cartwright wrote the first set of rules for the game. There would be nine players on each of two teams. Three strikes would be an out. The bases would be 90 feet apart.

The first recorded game took place in Hoboken, New Jersey, on June 19, 1846. The Knickerbocker Baseball Club of New York played the New York Nine. The Knickerbockers lost 23 to 1! That game **resembled** today's games. There was a pitcher, a catcher, four infielders, and three outfielders. The object of the game was to score more runs than the other team.

Throughout the 1800s, baseball became more and more **popular.** It seemed that everyone wanted to play the game or watch others play it. But a **conflict** soon developed. Some people wanted baseball to be an amateur sport. Others wanted it to be played by **professionals.** In that case, the players would be paid. This would allow them to make baseball their **careers.** Today's players sometimes earn a million dollars or more in a season. Baseball today is big business.

Why do you think baseball is such a popular sport in the United States?

_____

_____

_____

Vocabulary: Meaning and Message. © Fearon/Janus Publishers

Using Context

Name _____ Date _____

Choose a word from the box to replace the highlighted words in each sentence.

completed	popular	resembled	reliable	origin
professionals	research	career	regard	conflict

1. I didn't know the history, so I did some **careful study of the facts** in the library. _____

2. It is often difficult to know the true **beginnings** of a sport.

   _____

3. If there's something you like to do, you might try to make a **life's work or business** of it. _____

4. Major league ball players are considered **people who get paid for work that requires much education and training.**

   _____

5. Some people **think of** Babe Ruth as the best ball player ever.

   _____

6. Those who show up on time and do their best are considered **dependable** players. _____

7. I might not know how hard the test is until I have **finished** it.

   _____

8. It seems that everyone loves baseball. It is an extremely **well-liked** sport. _____

9. Hammer took his name from the baseball player Hammerin' Hank Aaron. People felt the two men **were similar to** each other.

   _____

10. Newspaper stories about what took place in the game's ninth inning are in **strong disagreement.** _____

Vocabulary Development: Exact Meaning

Name _____   Date _____

As you know, a synonym is a word that has the same or nearly the same meaning as another word. However, most synonyms don't have *exactly* the same meanings. Sometimes one synonym can be used for another. But it doesn't always work. For example, consider the word *talk*. Synonyms for *talk* include: *communicate, argue, converse, rap, consult, gossip, chatter,* and *jabber*. All describe the act of talking. But would you rather be described as someone who *talks* or as someone who *jabbers* or *chatters?* A *chatterer* talks quickly and doesn't stop talking. A *jabberer* talks quickly and is impossible to understand. Other synonyms of talk can be used in different situations. They each describe a certain kind of talking.

Many words in the English language have synonyms. Try to be clear and exact when you use them. Choose the words that best express your ideas. Your dictionary and thesaurus can help you.

Write two synonyms for each word below. Then use each synonym in a separate sentence.

A. regard _____   _____

1. _____

_____

2. _____

_____

Vocabulary Development: Exact Meaning

Name _____ Date _____

B. origin _____ _____

1. _____

    _____

2. _____

    _____

C. conflict _____ _____

1. _____

    _____

2. _____

    _____

D. complete _____ _____

1. _____

    _____

2. _____

    _____

E. reliable _____ _____

1. _____

    _____

2. _____

    _____

Puzzle

Name _____ Date _____

Use the clues to help you complete the crossword puzzle. The answers can be found in the box.

research   resemble   origin   reliable   career
professional   popular   regarded   conflict   completed

Across

1. one's lifetime work or business
5. a highly skilled person
7. considered; thought to be
8. study; investigation
9. argument; battle

Down

1. finished; made final
2. the beginning of something; source
3. able to be trusted
4. liked by many
6. to be similar to something else

Vocabulary: Meaning and Message © Fearon/Janus Publishers

Lesson 4, Exercise 5
Word Power: Connectors

Name _____ Date _____

Conjunctions and **prepositions** are parts of speech.

A **conjunction** is a word that joins other words or groups of words. In a dictionary, the word *conjunction* is usually abbreviated as *conj.* Here are some common conjunctions:

      and   but   or   nor   for   so   yet

Here are some examples of conjunctions used in sentences:

Baseball is popular *and* competitive.

We got to the staduim, *but* the game had ended.

Yolanda enjoys baseball, *so* her brother bought her a glove.

A. Choose one of the conjunctions above to complete each sentence below.

1. Our team will play either today _____ tomorrow.

2. I called you, _____ you weren't home.

3. I am tired, _____ I am also happy.

4. He never went there, _____ does he plan to.

5. It started raining, _____ the game was cancelled.

6. She was sad _____ lonely.

7. We must leave now, _____ it is getting late.

A **preposition** shows shows how a noun or pronoun and another word in a sentence are related. In a dictionary, the word *preposition* is usually abbreviated as *prep.* Here are some common prepositions:

    of   at   with   by   from   on   in   into   off

Here are some examples of prepositions used in sentences:

We walked *around* the stadium.

The ball went *across* the foul line, *over* the wall, and *into* the stands.

He walked *through* the parking lot *to* his car.

B. Use each of these prepositions in a sentence of your own. Write your sentences on a separate sheet of paper.

near	**without**	**under**

Writing on Your Own

Name _____ Date _____

Suppose you write a sports column for your school newspaper. Recently, many students have written to you. Some have said that sports are dangerous and too competitive. They think sports shouldn't be played at school. But others say that sports are important. These students want to see even more sports programs at school. What do you think? First, list the positive things you could say about sports.

_____

_____

_____

_____

_____

Now list the negative things you could say about sports.

_____

_____

_____

_____

_____

Decide how you feel about the question. What is your opinion?

_____

_____

Now write your column on a separate sheet of paper. In it, tell both the good and the bad sides of having sports be a part of school life. Give your opinion, based on the information you have presented. Try to make your argument as strong and clear as you can. Correct any errors and write a final draft. You might want to read your column to others in your class. Do your classmates agree with you?

Vocabulary: Meaning and Message © Fearon/Janus Publishers

Test

Name _____ Date _____

Choose the best word to complete each sentence.

1. You can _____ it as an unimportant matter.

   A. reliable   B. resemble   C. regard   D. complete

2. The major leagues keep _____ records of each game played.

   A. conflicted   B. reliable   C. competitive   D. career

3. The World Series games are the year's most _____.

   A. reliable   B. researched   C. resembled   D. popular

4. Most professional ball players began their _____ in the minor leagues. Then they went on to the major leagues.

   A. careers   B. origins   C. conflicts   D. competitions

5. Among sports writers, there is _____ about who is the greatest ball player.

   A. origin   B. competitive   C. conflict   D. career

6. He trained long and hard to become a _____.

   A. amateur   B. professional   C. research   D. complete

7. Baseball seems to have had its _____ in the United States.

   A. career   B. origin   C. competition   D. research

8. When each task is done, the job will be _____.

   A. original   B. professional   C. completed   D. conflict

9. In some ways, baseball _____ cricket.

   A. resembles   B. conflicts   C. regards   D. relies on

10. I'll go to the library to _____ the game's origins.

    A. conflict   B. research   C. compete   D. career

Unit 4 Review

Name _____ Date _____

A. Choose the word or phrase that is similar in meaning to the highlighted word. Darken the circled letter beside the word.

1. **reliable** information
   - Ⓐ able to be trusted
   - Ⓑ not worthy
   - Ⓒ conflicting
   - Ⓓ incredible

2. **unnecessary** noise
   - Ⓐ wanted
   - Ⓑ violent
   - Ⓒ not needed
   - Ⓓ anticipated

3. **dissatisfied** buyer
   - Ⓐ pleased
   - Ⓑ not pleased
   - Ⓒ expensive
   - Ⓓ unlucky

4. **irrelevant** information
   - Ⓐ necessary
   - Ⓑ funny
   - Ⓒ complicated
   - Ⓓ not important

5. **inexpensive** dress
   - Ⓐ low-priced
   - Ⓑ high-priced
   - Ⓒ large
   - Ⓓ popular

6. busy **schedule**
   - Ⓐ achievement
   - Ⓑ performance
   - Ⓒ list of events
   - Ⓓ evening

7. **complicated** directions
   - Ⓐ complex
   - Ⓑ simple
   - Ⓒ inexpensive
   - Ⓓ unnecessary

8. **incredible** story
   - Ⓐ sad
   - Ⓑ complicated
   - Ⓒ irrelevant
   - Ⓓ hard to believe

9. excellent **performance**
   - Ⓐ show
   - Ⓑ study
   - Ⓒ career
   - Ⓓ decision

10. great **achievement**
    - Ⓐ performance
    - Ⓑ debate
    - Ⓒ accomplishment
    - Ⓓ schedule

11. **favorite** movie
    - Ⓐ best liked
    - Ⓑ least liked
    - Ⓒ scariest
    - Ⓓ most expensive

12. strong **conflict**
    - Ⓐ disagreement
    - Ⓑ schedule
    - Ⓒ competition
    - Ⓓ research

13. **tremendous** amount
    - Ⓐ very large
    - Ⓑ tiny
    - Ⓒ unnecessary
    - Ⓓ complicated

14. **especially** happy
    - Ⓐ soon
    - Ⓑ very
    - Ⓒ professionally
    - Ⓓ slightly

Vocabulary: Meaning and Message © Fearon/Janus Publishers

Unit 4 Review

Name _____ Date _____

B. Choose the letter of the word or phrase that is similar in
meaning to the highlighted word. Darken the circled letter
beside the word.

1. **fierce**
   - Ⓐ wild
   - Ⓑ athletic
   - Ⓒ popular
   - Ⓓ individual

2. **cooperation**
   - Ⓐ competition
   - Ⓑ anticipation
   - Ⓒ individual
   - Ⓓ working together

3. **regulations**
   - Ⓐ statements
   - Ⓑ rules
   - Ⓒ schedules
   - Ⓓ trouble

4. **qualify**
   - Ⓐ argue about
   - Ⓑ anticipate
   - Ⓒ be fit for
   - Ⓓ leave out

5. **anticipation**
   - Ⓐ disagreeing
   - Ⓑ belief
   - Ⓒ expectation
   - Ⓓ appreciation

6. **career**
   - Ⓐ controversy
   - Ⓑ commitment
   - Ⓒ professional
   - Ⓓ life's work

7. **certainly**
   - Ⓐ although
   - Ⓑ tremendously
   - Ⓒ surely
   - Ⓓ popular

8. **disagree**
   - Ⓐ think differently
   - Ⓑ surround
   - Ⓒ resemble
   - Ⓓ regard

9. **origin**
   - Ⓐ conflict
   - Ⓑ beginning
   - Ⓒ research
   - Ⓓ statement

10. **research**
    - Ⓐ conflict
    - Ⓑ study
    - Ⓒ commitment
    - Ⓓ individual

11. **represent**
    - Ⓐ stand for
    - Ⓑ qualify
    - Ⓒ appoint
    - Ⓓ elect

12. **increase**
    - Ⓐ become smaller
    - Ⓑ measure
    - Ⓒ minimum
    - Ⓓ become larger

13. **completed**
    - Ⓐ begun
    - Ⓑ old
    - Ⓒ finished
    - Ⓓ dissatisfied

Glossary

A _____

a chieve ment (ə chēv′ mənt) **noun,** something accomplished

a dopt (ə dopt′) **verb, 1.** to take into one's family and raise as one's own **2.** to take or use as one's own

ad vice (ad vīs′) **noun,** an idea given to help solve a problem

af fect (ə fekt′) **verb, 1.** to produce a change in **2.** to move the emotions of

air plane (âr plān′) **noun,** a heavier-than-air vehicle that has an engine and that flies

al ly (al′ ī *for noun;* ə lī′ *for verb*) **noun,** a person or country joined with others for a common purpose—**verb,** to join with others for a common purpose

al though (ôl thō′) **conjunction,** in spite of the fact that

an tic i pa tion (an tis ə pa shən) **noun,** the act of expecting

ap pli ance (əplī′ əns) **noun,** a device, usually run by electricity, that performs a specific task

ap point (ə point′) **verb,** to select for a position

ap pre ci ate (ə prē′ shē āt′) **verb, 1.** to recognize the value of **2.** to be grateful or thankful for

ar e a (âr′ ē ə) **noun, 1.** the measurement of a surface **2.** a space or section usually having a specific use, such as the dining *area* **3.** a field of interest or study

ath let ic (ath let′ ik) **adjective,** of or having to do with a person trained in sports

at ti tude (at′ i tūd′) **noun,** a way of acting, thinking, or feeling

B _____

bank book (bangk′ buk) **noun,** a record of money deposited or taken out of a savings account

be lief (bi lēf′) **noun,** the feeling that something is true or real

bi cy cle (bī′ si kəl) **noun,** a vehicle with a seat and two wheels, one behind the other. A bicycle has handlebars for steering and two foot pedals that turn the wheels and move the bicycle along

blend (blend) **verb,** to mix well—**noun,** a mixture

bod y (bod′ ē) **noun, 1.** the physical structure of a person or animal **2.** a group of people or things

break fast (brek′ fəst) **noun,** the first meal of the day

breathe (brē*th*) **verb,** to bring air into the lungs and then let it out

busi ness (biz′ nis) **noun, 1.** work done to make money **2.** the buying and selling of things **3.** activities or affairs

C _____

ca reer (kə rîr′) **noun,** life's work or business

cau tion (kô′ shən) **noun, 1.** a warning **2.** great care—**verb,** to warn

cer tain ly (sûr′ tən lē) **adverb,** surely

charge ac count (chärj′ ə kount′) **noun,** a business arrangement that allows one to buy things and pay for them at a certain later date

check ing ac count (chek′ ing ə kount′) **noun,** a bank account that allows one to take out money from his or her account by writing out checks

coast (kōst) **noun,** seashore, land next to the sea—**verb,** to slide or glide along without any effort

com mit ment (kə mit′ mənt) **noun,** the act of promising to do something

com pe ti tion (kom′ pi tish′ ən) **noun,** the act of trying to win against others

com plete (kəm plēt′) **adjective,** whole or entire—**verb,** to finish

com pli cate (kom′ pli kāt′) **verb,** to make difficult to understand

con flict (kon′ flikt *for noun;* kən flikt′ *for verb*) **noun, 1.** a long fight or war **2.** a strong disagreement—**verb,** to disagree strongly

con science (kon′ shəns) **noun,** a feeling of what is right and wrong

con sid er (kən sid′ ər) **verb, 1.** to think carefully about something in order to help decide **2.** to be thoughtful and respectful **3.** to regard as **4.** to take into account, to keep in mind

con tro ver sial (kon′ trə vûr′ shəl) **adjective,** open to disagreement

cook book (kŭk′ bŭk) **noun,** a book that has recipes and other information about food

co op er a tion (kō op′ ə rā′shən) **noun,** the act of working together

cred it card (kred′ it kard) **noun,** a card given by a store or bank that permits one to buy things and pay for them later

D _____

de gree (di grē′) **noun, 1.** a unit or number used to measure temperature **2.** amount or extent **3.** a title given by a school to those who have completed a certain course of study

de moc ra cy (di mok′ rə sē) **noun,** a form of government in which the people being governed have ruling power

de pos it (di poz′ it) **verb, 1.** to put money or valuables in a bank—**noun, 1.** something put in a bank or other place for safekeeping **2.** part of the whole payment

dic ta tor ship (dik tā′ tər ship) **noun,** the state of being ruled by a person or small group with total control

di ges tive (di jes′ tiv) **adjective,** relating to the process of breaking down food so that it can be used by the body

din ner (din′ ər) **noun,** the main meal of the day

dis a gree (dis′ ə grē′) **verb, 1.** to differ in opinion **2.** to argue

dis crim i na tion (di skrim′ ə nā′ shən) **noun,** to treat people unfairly because of their background

dish wash er (dish′ wôsh′ ər) **noun,** an appliance used to wash and dry dishes, pots and pans, and utensils

dis sat is fied (dis sat′ is fīd′) **adjective,** not pleased

dry er (drī′ ər) **noun,** an appliance used to dry something

due date (dü′ dāt) **noun,** the month, day, and year that the last payment for something must be made

E _____

ear (îr) **noun,** the organ of the body that enables one to hear

ed u ca tion (ej′ ə kā′ shən) **noun,** the act of developing knowledge

e lec tion (i lek′ shən) **noun,** the act of choosing by voting

e lec tric i ty (i lik tris′ i tē) **noun, 1.** a basic form of energy **2.** an electric current

el e va tor (el′ ə vā′ tər) **noun,** a small room, cage, or boxlike structure that raises and lowers people and things

em ploy ee (em′ ploi ē′) **noun,** a person who works for another for pay

em ploy er (em ploi′ ər) **noun,** a person or business who pays others to work

e qual i ty (i kwol′ i tē) **noun,** the condition of being the same in value, quantity, size, or amount

e soph a gus (i sof′ ə gəs) **noun,** a tube from the throat to the stomach through which food travels

es pe cial ly (e spesh′ ə lē) **adverb,** to a great degree; more than usual

ex pe ri ence (ek spîr′ ē əns) **noun, 1.** living through or seeing an event **2.** the knowledge gained from having lived through events—**verb,** to undergo, participate in, feel

eye (ī) **noun, 1.** the organ that enables people and animals to see **2.** the pigmented, or colored, part of the eye: the iris **3.** the part of the face that includes the eyelid, eyebrows, and eyelashes **4.** a look **5.** anything that is like an eye in appearance or use **6.** the calm at the center of a hurricane—**verb,** to look carefully at

F _____

Fahr en heit (fər′ ən hīt′) **adjective,** a temperature scale on which water freezes at 32 degrees and boils at 212 degrees

fa vor ite (fā′ vər it) **adjective,** liked best; especially liked

fer ry (fer′ ē) **noun,** a boat that takes people, cars, and goods across a body of water—**verb,** to cross or carry by ferry

fierce (fîrs) **adjective, 1.** intense **2.** likely to attack **3.** wild

for mer ly (fôr′ mər lē) **adverb,** once; in the past

free dom (frē′ dəm) **noun,** the condition of being able to do what one wants

G _____

gov ern ment (guv′ ərn mənt) **noun, 1.** all the people in charge of ruling a city, state, country, or other place **2.** the system of ruling or governing

---

at; ate; tär; shâre; end; wē; in; ice; fierce; not; sō; lông; oil; out; up; ūse; trüe; pùt; bûrn; chew; wing; shoe; both; mother; hw in which; zh in treasure; ə in about, agent, pencil, collect, focus

H

hand (hand) **noun, 1.** the part of the arm from the wrist down, made up of a thumb, four fingers, and a palm **2.** a pointer, as on a clock **3.** clapping or applause **4.** a side or direction, as in "on the *right-hand* page" **5.** a person who is part of a crew or group **6.** help or assistance **7.** one round of a card game **8.** the cards held by a person at a certain time—**verb,** to pass or give with the hand

hor i zon tal (hôr′ ə zon′ təl) **adjective,** parallel to the horizon; flat, even, and straight across

I

il le gal (i lē′ gəl) **adjective,** not legal; against the law

im peach′ ment (im pēch mənt) **noun,** the act of bringing charges of wrongdoing against a public official

im por tant (im pôr′ tənt) **adjective, 1.** something that means a great deal; of great value **2.** having great power or high position

im prop er (im prop′ ər) **adjective, 1.** wrong; incorrect **2.** in bad taste

in ci dent (in′ si dənt) **noun,** event; happening

in crease (in krēs′, *for verb;* in′ krēs, *for noun*) **verb,** to become larger in size, amount, or degree—**noun,** the amount by which something is made larger

in cred i ble (in kred′ ə bəl) **adjective, 1.** hard to believe **2.** amazing

in di vid u al (in′ də vij′ ü əl) **adjective,** for one person—**noun,** a single person or thing

in ex pen sive (in′ ek spen′ siv) **adjective,** not costly

in gre di ent (in grē′ dē ənt) **noun,** any of the parts of a mixture

in ter na tion al (in′ tər nash′ ə nəl) **adjective,** of two or more countries

in tes tine (in tes′ tin) **noun,** a long tube extending from the stomach, used in the digestive process. It is divided into the small and large intestine.

in ves ti ga tion (in ves′ ti gā′ shən) **noun,** the act of looking carefully into something to discover the truth

ir rel e vant (ir rel′ ə vənt) **adjective,** not relevant; not relating to the point or subject

L

lay a way (lā′ ə wā′) **noun,** a way of buying, in which part of the money is put down and the item is put aside until all the payments have been made

length (lengkth *or* length) **noun, 1.** a measure of how long something is **2.** the extent of something from start to finish **3.** a piece of something

M

max i mum (mak′ sə məm) **noun, 1.** the greatest number or amount possible **2.** the highest point or degree recorded or reached—**adjective,** the greatest possible

min i mum (min′ ə məm) **noun, 1.** the smallest number or amount possible **2.** the lowest point or number recorded or reached—**adjective,** the lowest or smallest

mis un der stand (mis′ un dər stand′) **verb,** to not understand something correctly; to form or have the wrong idea about something

mis use (mis ūs′ *for noun;* mis ūz′ *for verb*) **noun,** wrong use—**verb,** to use wrongly

month (munth) **noun,** one of the twelve parts of a year

mo tor cy cle (mō′ tər sī′ kəl) **noun,** a motor-powered vehicle with two wheels that is larger and heavier than a bicycle

mouth (mouth, *for noun;* mouth *for verb*) **noun, 1.** the opening in the body that contains teeth and a tongue and through which food is taken in **2.** an opening that is like a mouth—**verb,** to say in an insincere or false way

mus cle (mus′ əl) **noun, 1.** a tissue in the body's organs that can be tightened or relaxed to make the body move **2.** strength

O

of fi cial (ə fish′ əl) **adjective, 1.** by authority **2.** done in a formal way—**noun,** a person holding an office or position

op po site (op′ ə zit *or* op ə sit) **adjective, 1.** on the other side or end from someone or something, facing **2.** totally different—**noun,** anyone or anything that is totally different from someone or something else

or gan (ôr gən) **noun, 1.** a part of a person or animal that is made up of tissues and does a specific job **2.** a musical instrument with pipes of different lengths and one or more keyboards

or gan ize (ôr gə nīz′) **verb, 1.** to arrange things in an orderly way; to plan **2.** to make **3.** to form into a group

or i gin (ôr i jin *or* or i jin) **noun,** the beginning of something

ov en (uv′ ən) **noun,** an enclosed space in which food can be baked, heated, or roasted

P _____

pay ment (pā′ mənt) **noun, 1.** the act of paying **2.** something that is paid

per form ance (pər fôr′ məns) **noun,** a show or other presentation before an audience

po lit i cal par ty (pə lit′ i kəl par′ te) **noun,** a group through which people can express ideas about the government

pop u lar (pop′ yə lər) **adjective,** liked by many

prej u dice (prej′ ə dis) **noun,** an opinion formed before all the facts are known

pres ence (prez′ əns) **noun,** the fact of being at some place at some time

prin ci ple (prin′ sə pəl) **noun, 1.** a basic truth or law **2.** a rule of conduct

pro fes sion al (prə fesh′ ə nəl) **adjective,** working at a profession—**noun,** a person who does work that requires special education

Q _____

qual i fy (kwäl′ ə fī′) **verb,** to be fit or eligible for something

R _____

re cent (rē′ sēnt) **adjective,** new; done, made, or happening in a time just before now

rec i pe (res′ ə pē′) **noun,** a list of food items and the directions for making a kind of food or drink

rec tan gle (rek′ tang′ gəl) **noun,** a four-sided figure with four right angles

re frig er a tor (ri frij′ ə rā′ tər) **noun,** an appliance or room with a cooling system that keeps food and drinks from spoiling

re gard (ri gärd) **verb,** consider, think about, look at

reg u la tion (reg′ yə lā′ shən) **noun,** a law or rule

re li a ble (ri lī′ ə bəl) **adjective,** able to be depended on

rep re sent (rep′ ri zent′) **verb, 1.** to act or speak for **2.** to be a sign or symbol for

re search (ri sûrch′ or rē′ surch) **noun,** a careful study to find out the facts—**verb,** to study carefully

re sem ble (ri zem′ bəl) **verb,** to be like or similar to

S _____

sa li va (sə lī′ və) **noun,** the clear liquid inside the mouth that begins the digestive process and that helps in chewing

sav ings (sā′ vingz) **noun,** money saved

scan dal (skan′ dəl) **noun,** an act that shocks people and that usually brings disgrace to those involved

sched ule (skej′ ül) **noun,** a list of the times when certain things will happen or be done

sense (sens) **noun, 1.** any of the five functions of hearing, sight, taste, smell, and touch **2.** feeling or impression—**verb,** to feel or understand

sig na ture (sig′ nə chər) **noun,** the hand-written name of a person written by that person

sim i lar (sim′ ə lər) **adjective,** alike, but having some differences

skin (skin) **noun, 1.** the outer covering of a person's body **2.** something like skin in looks or use—**verb,** to remove the skin from

sol id (sol′ id) **adjective, 1.** firm, hard **2.** filled throughout, not hollow **3.** having no breaks or interruptions **4.** strong and dependable **5.** having the same color or material throughout **6.** having length, width, and thickness—**noun, 1.** a thing that is solid, not liquid or gas **2.** an object that has length, width, and thickness

sound (sound) **noun,** that which can be heard—**verb, 1.** to cause or produce a noise **2.** to pronounce or be pronounced

square feet (skwâr fēt) **noun, plural,** a measure of the total area of a figure

state ment (stāt′ mənt) **noun,** something shown or explained in words

stom ach (stum′ ək) **noun,** the area between the esophagus and the small intestine where food is received and broken down—**verb,** to bear, endure, be patient about

stove (stōv) **noun,** a metal object used for heating and cooking

sub way (sub′ wā) **noun,** a train powered by electricity that runs under the streets of a city

sur round (sə round′) **verb,** to form a circle around

---

at; ate; tär; shâre; end; wē; in; ice; fîerce; not; sō; lông; oil; out; up; ūse; trüe; put; bûrn; chew; wing; shoe; both; mother;
hw in which; **zh** in treasure; ə in about, agent, pencil, collect, focus

sys tem (sis´ t əm) **noun, 1.** a set of laws, rules, facts, or beliefs **2.** an orderly method

T

taste (tāst) **noun, 1.** the sense by which flavors are noticed in the mouth **2.** a specific flavor that is taken into the mouth. Bitter, sour, salty, and sweet and the four basic tastes. **3.** a small amount put into one's mouth **4.** a liking or appreciation—**verb, 1.** to recognize flavors by the sense of taste **2.** to put a little into one's mouth to test the flavor

tax i (tak´ sē) **noun,** a car whose driver you pay to take you somewhere

tem per a ture (tem´ pər ə chər) **noun,** how hot or cold something is, measured by a thermometer

ther mom e ter (thər mom´ i tər) **noun,** a device used to measure temperature

toas ter (tōs´ tər) **noun,** a small appliance that warms and browns bread

tongue (tung) **noun, 1.** the fleshy, movable piece attached to the floor of the mouth, used for tasting and to help in speaking **2.** a language **3.** something like a tongue in shape or use, such as the material that is under the laces of a shoe

tooth (tüth) —*plural: teeth*— **noun,** any of the hard bonelike parts in the mouth, used for biting and chewing.

top ic (top´ ik) **noun,** the subject of a speech, paper, or discussion

traf fic (traf´ ik) **noun, 1.** vehicles moving along a route **2.** the buying and selling of items, often of an illegal kind; trade—**verb,** to buy or sell, especially illegally

trans por ta tion (trans´ pər tā´ shən) **noun,** the means or system of moving or carrying something from one place to another

trav el (trav´ əl) **verb,** to make a journey; to go from one place to another

tre men dous (tri men´ dəs) **adjective,** enormous; huge; very large

tri al (trī´ əl) **noun,** the examination of the facts by a court of law to decide the truth of a charge

trou ble (trub´ əl) **noun,** a difficult, distressing, or annoying situation—**verb,** to disturb or annoy

U

un con sti tu tion al (un´ kon sti tü´ shə nəl *or* un´ kon sti tū´ shə nal) **adjective,** not in keeping with a constitution, especially the United States Constitution

un im por tant (un´ im pôr´ tənt) **adjective,** not important; of little matter or concern

un nec es sar y (un nes´ ə ser´ ē) **adjective,** not necessary; not needed

V

ve hi cle (vē´ i kəl) **noun,** any device used to carry people or objects. Cars, ferries, airplanes, motorcycles, and bicycles are vehicles.

ver ti cal (vûr´ ti kəl) **adjective,** upright, straight up and down

W

wash er (wôsh´ ər) **noun, 1.** a machine that uses water to get clothes clean **2.** a person who washes **3.** a flat metal ring used between a nut and bolt to provide a tighter fit

width (width) **noun,** the distance from one side of a thing to another

Y

year ly (yîr´ lē) **adjective, 1.** done or occurring once every 12 months **2.** measured by the year—**adverb,** every year